FREEDOM ROAD

Harold Hough

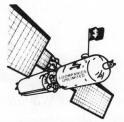

**Loompanics Unlimited
Port Townsend, Washington**

FREEDOM ROAD
© 1991 by Harold Hough
Printed in USA

Published by:
Loompanics Unlimited   796.5
PO Box 1197
Port Townsend, WA 98368

Cover and Illustrations by Barbara Williams

ISBN 1-55950-067-0
Library of Congress
    Catalog Card Number Pending

Dedicated To:

Ellen, Tiffany, Pasha, Tom, Clifford, Penny, Barry, Julie, Victor, Janet, Jeanie, and Evie.

Thanks for sharing Freedom Road with me and making my life happy.

Contents

Introduction

"Only our individual faith in freedom can keep us free."

— **Dwight D. Eisenhower**

Many years ago, I had serious financial problems. In fact, they were so bad I couldn't afford the down payment for a house or the deposit for an apartment. I was faced with the real possibility of having no place to live. But I wasn't the typical homeless person who couldn't find a job or fell through the holes of the government "safety net." No, I was one of the people paying taxes and working.

How could this happen? I played the game according to the rules. I wore three piece suits to work, drove a nice car, used credit cards, lived in a major metropolitan area, and made more money than the average person. Yet, I was broke, miserable, overweight, stressed, and well on the way to an ulcer. Even the neighbors and government were dictating how I should live. Was this the great American Dream everybody talked about?

During my spare time, I started to dream about a different life where I escaped the problems of daily life, lived in the unspoiled wilderness, and was unshackled from the politicians and neighbors who wanted to dictate every part of my life.

But, instead of just dreaming, I changed my life. I started a new job where I could cut costs and avoid the hassles of my previous job. I started to write articles for small publications. I battled my way out of debt. Soon there was nothing holding me back. My wife and I bought a recreational vehicle and took off down the road.

Today, we are happier than we could have ever guessed when we left. I've gone from an overweight, middle-aged executive to a thin person who looks like he just turned thirty. My wife, who has lupus, is taking less medicine and surprising the doctor with her dramatic improvement. We even have a better marriage with fewer arguments than before.

The wonderful tonic that has given us health and happiness can be found with a Recreational Vehicle (RV) and any open road. We left the stress of a regular life behind in the city and started living a simpler lifestyle where happiness is better than status and government is left for others to deal with.

You will probably ask one question while reading this book, "What if everybody was lazy and lived this way?" Aren't we just parasites living on the productivity of others? That's a fair question, but I have an answer.

Before I started living the Freedom Road lifestyle, I worked for defense contractors. The government paid hundreds of thousands of dollars for the reports I wrote. Ninety percent of them were filed and never read (except for the executive summary). Today, I write articles that are read and enjoyed by thousands of readers, although they only cost hundreds of dollars. Not only are my articles better and cheaper, I enjoy the work much more.

What would happen if people worked at jobs they liked while providing better and cheaper products? Prices would drop like a rock, people *would* have the time to enjoy life, salesmen selling blood pressure medicine would probably have to find new employment, and government revenues would wither away. That's a peaceful revolution I want to be a part of.

So, if the pressures of society and government are weighing you down and you're looking for a better life, sit back, open your mind, and take the first step on Freedom Road.

1

The Modern Pioneers

"Individuality is the aim of political liberty."

— **James Fenimore Cooper**

Nothing defined the American character more than the Western Movement. The hardships encountered in a new land nourished a streak of individuality still with us. In fact, it's our reverence for the individual that characterizes America and binds us together more closely than ethnic background.

The pioneer movement started centuries ago, when the first settlers boarded ships in England, and still exists in the wilds of Alaska where families carve homesteads from the wilderness. Even though most people have "settled down," that spirit still lives in our disdain for authority, the lure of an open road, and our love of the Old West.

What drove us across the continent? It wasn't gold. Gold never brought many people over from Europe to the English colonies. It didn't lure people across the Allegheny Mountains. It didn't call men to fight in Texas, either. True, gold helped open California, Alaska, and Colorado, but most of the pioneers weren't prospectors. Nor were they looking for land. Land was still available in the East and many even sold their farms in order to move west.

These settlers were searching for freedom and the chance to make a new life for themselves. They wanted freedom from government, freedom from community standards, freedom from past mistakes and, most of all, freedom to be judged for what they were. These were people who didn't like traditional society and wanted to live without its restrictions.

The West was also a new land and a new beginning. Nobody really cared if you were a drunken son of a duke or somebody who had tangled with the law. A person was judged by what he had done out West, not past mistakes. The past was forgotten.

One example of the West's tolerance for previous failure is the tale of a young man who in the early part of the 1800s built a promising political career and even was mentioned as a possible presidential candidate. His political future, however, was ruined by killing a rival in a duel, drinking, and a short unhappy marriage with a socially prominent wife. In disgrace he left society and lived with the Indians before leaving for Mexico. There, he joined the Texas Independence movement, became the leader of their army, and captured Santa Anna at the battle of San Jacinto. He became the President of the Republic of Texas and died a widely respected man. His name was Sam Houston.

Today Sam Houston would be a failure. Who would give a job or credit to a man who had killed someone, drank excessively, was divorced, and had "dropped out" to live with savages for many years? Even if he did manage to keep a house and job, he would have problems living in a world where long grass and improperly painted houses are considered crimes.

The West was a pressure release valve that gave new lives to decent people who didn't want to be judged by conventional standards. Most settled down in communities with other nonconformists and adopted laws that gave them the freedom they wanted. To others, however, these few laws were too much and they left for new horizons. The West's history is filled with the names of people who spearheaded a movement into the west only to move on when the area got civilized. The prospectors in the musical, *Paint Your Wagon* were reflections of real people who moved on as soon as civilization caught up with them. One such example was Schifflen, who founded Tombstone, Arizona, and then moved north to be part of the Klondike Gold Rush.

So what happens to the modern person who doesn't cut his grass regularly, keeps an unlicensed car in his driveway or doesn't want to consult his zoning board when he paints his house? In most cases he shuts up and plays the game. He marches off like a good little soldier to work, engages in the petty games of big business during the day, comes home and cuts the grass, spends Saturday fixing up the house, and then treats himself to a beer and a football game on Sunday. His love of freedom and individuality has been repressed and inevitably comes back to haunt him as an ulcer.

Others try to fight the system. They ignore petty laws and are hounded by police and neighbors trying to force their standards on others. The result is an endless stream of fines and jailings that are meted out to nonconformists by society; Sam Houston, Thomas Paine, Daniel Boone, Henry Thoreau, and Benjamin Franklin would have ended up in the same place. Inevitably, their lives are destroyed or they surrender to the government. The battle for freedom has lost another soldier.

There is another way for the freedom loving individual to keep his beliefs without compromising his principles. It's the same solution that sent the Europeans to the Colonies, sent colonists to the Northwest Territory, sent Midwesterners to California, and Californians to Alaska: move from the hassles of everyday life.

The pioneer spirit that forged our national identity is still alive in the recreational vehicle community. For some people, it's the weekend compromise with our modern world stealing a few days from conventional behavior. For many it's a reward for a life of conventional work, a retirement lifestyle that keeps both the body and mind young. But, for some it's not a compromise with modern society, but a declaration of independence from the world around them. They are the modern pioneers — moving to new lands that promise a better and freer life.

The full time RVer (young or old) is the last link to our pioneer ancestors. They aren't afraid of change and even relish it. They are self-sufficient and willing to stand on their own feet. They judge you on your own merits, not the size of your rig. They exhibit a distrust of the restrictions of modern society, and they have a vitality and friendliness that makes them more interesting than most people.

RV living isn't new. Some Americans have been living a nomadic existence for over half a century. They raised families and become grandparents without the anchor of a house or a conventional job. They were the real pioneers, living in makeshift trailers and living with the stigma associated with nomadic life.

Today things have changed. The snowbird phenomenon has given RVs acceptability. Many communities cater to RVs and the business they bring while the RV builders now make machines that allow us to live in the wilderness while enjoying TV, microwave ovens, and air conditioning.

So life on the road isn't a trail of hardships. It's a way to enjoy life to its fullest while avoiding the entanglements of our modern world. If you treasure your freedom as our forefathers did, join us on Freedom Road.

2

What Is Freedom?
Can RVs Help?

"(I am) lord of myself, accountable to none."

— **Benjamin Franklin**

Freedom is a word often used, but rarely understood. We frequently hear oppressed people crying for freedom, but most of the time, they only want someone of their own race to lead them. Usually, they only trade one tyrant for another.

Then there is the freedom social workers speak of: freedom from hunger, cold, and illness. But are these really freedoms or just a trap to strip us of our rights? Since we are all subject to the physical constraints of hunger, illness, and cold, government can assert that no one is truly free and therefore any depredation visited on its citizens is justified because they weren't free anyway.

Those who speak of freedom from hunger also set another snare, because they can then justify stealing other freedoms once considered our inalienable rights. For instance, the Supreme Court could rule that freedom of speech should be limited if it interferes with another's freedom from hunger. You may think this is ridiculous, but the courts are already using this line of thought to strip the Bill of Rights of any meaning. If we follow this through to the logical conclusion, we will only have the freedom to scavenge enough food to fill our bellies.

Others, especially the "Law and Order" group, speak of freedom from violence and the freedom to feel secure in your home. Usually this is a prelude to laws granting more police powers and fewer individual freedoms. The best answer to these people came over two hundred years ago at a meeting in a Richmond, Virginia, church where colonists were discussing how much freedom they should surrender for security. Suddenly a firebrand jumped up and gave an eloquent speech denouncing the idea. His words stirred the listeners and have lived throughout the ages, "Is life so dear and peace so sweet that it must be bought at the price of chains and slavery? God forbid it! I know not what course others may take, but as for me, give me liberty or give me death." Patrick Henry's words set the foundation of American thought: freedom cannot be traded for security.

If concepts like "Freedom From Hunger" are shams, what *is* freedom? In the Middle Ages it was something a ruler granted to the serfs. Freedoms weren't permanent and could be withdrawn at the monarch's pleasure. For instance, a generous ruler might waive his rights to spend the wedding night with a bride, in return for a cash payment. Such payments live today as marriage license fees, where you pay the government to recognize your marriage.

Fortunately, the Medieval concept of freedom disappeared along with the concept of divine right and absolute monarchy. The Age of Rousseau and Voltaire declared freedoms to be a birthright. This was most eloquently expressed by Thomas Jefferson in the Declaration of Independence, "We hold these truths to be self evident, that all men are created equal, that they are endowed by their creator with certain inalienable rights, that among these are life, liberty, and the pursuit of happiness. That to secure these rights, Governments are instituted among men, deriving their just powers from the consent of the governed." This was a new concept: rights belonged to each person and governments only existed to protect these rights. This conception of freedom continued for about one hundred and fifty years.

When the New Deal came, government growth started to intrude on the freedoms that the people enjoyed. The courts reacted to this challenge, not by enforcing our freedoms, but by arguing that the necessities of running the government required the curtailment of our freedoms. Once again, freedoms were granted by the government and could be taken away. We had come full circle.

Have we progressed in the last seven hundred years? No. Our freedoms are now recognized as grants to us by our government, not inherent rights. License laws and regulations concerning business tie us to our jobs as surely as the laws that bound the serf to the land. And finally, our lord and master, the government, takes more our labor and wealth than the absolute kings of old (anti-Semitic kings were considered tyrants because they would take 25% of the Jews' wealth).

We've seen the concept of freedom change and we know it means different things to different people. But what does freedom really imply? The dictionary is the simplest and most eloquent, "The absence of coercion or constraint in choice or action." Therefore, I define freedom as the ability to do what you want without coercion, as long as you do not coerce others. That is the type of freedom I sought and found in the world of RVs.

Freedom from Government

"Government is a kind of legalized pillage."

— **Elbert Hubbard**

There is only one type of coercion that really scares me. That is the power of the government. No matter who you are, they determine how you should behave until you die. If you fail to conform, they will fine or jail you at their wish. If you refuse, they have a police force that will gladly use weapons to bring you in, dead or alive.

Make no mistake about it, the government's use of force isn't just employed against violent criminals. We have all heard about police who use violence against the innocent or minor offenders. Usually the incidents are covered up with some lame excuse that the person was really guilty of breaking a minor law (like cursing the police officer while his head was being shoved into a wall). Trying to curb police excesses is seen as causing more crime. Inevitably, the only one to suffer is the person who got in the way of the police.

Can we ever be free from government interference? The best answer came from Skye d'Aureous and Natalee Hall in an early 1970s piece called "What If There Was a Millennium... and No One Came? or Don't Wait For an Engraved Invitation" (available in *Loompanics' Greatest Hits*). In this work, which was seminal in my understanding of freedom, they said the government will never abolish itself and just give you your freedom. In other words, if you are waiting for the government to give you an invitation to be free, you have a long wait. Although that may seem pessimistic, they also provide the answer to finding freedom. First, they tell us that the government and its coercive powers aren't everywhere. Therefore, you can find a place to practice your beliefs without instant government retaliation. Second, freedom is a scale ranging from total oppression to absolute freedom. That means you can achieve some freedom (according to your tastes) with only a small amount of effort.

This article tells us that, if you want freedom, you can't wait for it — you must act. But what actions will help us achieve that goal? Fortunately, bureaucracies are very rigid in their thinking and by analyzing their actions, we can avoid much of their pressure.

What we seek is freedom to ignore laws that affect our personal lives without restricting the freedom of other people. That means doing what we want without the threat of police interference. If we can avoid the police and their intrinsic threat of violence, we will have achieved our goal.

Fortunately, government is inherently incompetent and reacts in predictable ways. For instance, most law enforcement is reaction based. With the exception of a few "sting" operations, the police only act if they see something or someone reports the offense. That means if we remove ourselves from the police presence and their informers, they will never be able to react. And, since our expression of freedom doesn't hurt others, there is never a victim to make a complaint.

Most government laws and actions are based on the premise that all people live in fixed residences. Thinking this, they tax your real estate, fix its use through zoning, and control your behavior through silly laws. Without a fixed residence you can avoid most governments and many of their laws.

Finally, government enforcement is directed toward fixed residences. Draft notices come to your house through the mail. If your lawn isn't properly cut, the police visit you at your house. Just ask yourself what the draft board would do if they didn't have a place to send the induction notice and you didn't obediently surrender yourself to the authorities. Most likely they would just note the fact on a computer database so you could be apprehended if you're caught speeding (that's why law enforcement likes drunk driving road blocks). Again, the lack of a fixed residence and isolation from law enforcement gives you a great deal of freedom.

So basically, freedom from government can be acquired by avoiding law enforcement and their informers, and not owning a fixed residence. Of course, the police could become more innovative, but bloated bureaucracies discourage creativity. Besides, if they were innovative, they would have found a way to lessen violent crime with fewer taxes.

Freedom from Community Standards

"Our wretched species is so made that those who walk on the well-trodden path always throw stones at those who are showing a new road."

— **Voltaire**

Every neighborhood has one: a lettuce head who's the self-appointed protector of community standards. They are the type that walk up to you and say, "It looks like your lawn needs to be cut." Depending on your tolerance for such inane comments, your response may be a grunt or a wise crack. After all, he may think a well-mowed lawn is a thing of beauty, but you regard it as a nuisance and a poor substitute for wall-to-wall Astroturf.

Most libertarian-minded people usually ignore conformists and sometimes take perverse pleasure in bugging them. The problem occurs when this self-righteous snob is a politician or learns about a law that enforces his/her standards. Next thing you know, the police are knocking on your door and arresting you for "long grass" (don't laugh, it happens). You can try to fight them, but you know what they say about fighting city hall.

Most problems concerning community standards again come back to government force. If you want freedom from community standards, you must avoid places where government force can be used against you and try to live where people accept you as you are.

Freedom from Financial Concerns

"That man is the richest whose pleasures are the cheapest."

— **Henry David Thoreau**

Earlier in this chapter I said that freedom is the avoidance of coercion. In that respect, financial freedom isn't really a freedom because money doesn't force your actions. Instead, it just saps your resolve and encourages you to take actions you would rather avoid. It's more like a drug of modern society. We work at unpleasant tasks because we want to make more money. We spend too much money to advertise our wealth. We work ourselves into ill health to save for a retirement that is plagued by the ill health we contracted. And, when we've finally achieved that financial freedom we wasted our lives gaining, it's a millstone around our necks, forcing us to defend it from crooks and government. The Bible was correct when it admonished us to avoid the blind search for wealth.

Freedom comes from renouncing wealth and focusing on what our needs really are. No finer example of freedom through poverty can be found than Mahatma Gandhi. He spent much of his life travelling around British India wearing a few rags and eating little. As a consequence, he wasn't afraid of ignoring British taxes, violating British laws, and supporting his principles. After all, what were the British going to do to him? Send him to jail, give him three square meals a day and clothes? Maybe they could have confiscated his meager assets? In fact, they never found a way to handle him and he became a thorn in their side until independence and his untimely death.

I don't recommend such a ascetic lifestyle, but a change in our priorities would allow us to choose more interesting lines of work and even provide more freedom from the pillaging government.

Freedom Wrap-Up

"The only tyrant I accept in this world is the still voice within."

— **Mahatma Gandhi**

Freedom is achievable for each one of us if we only look at the impediments to freedom and act. As I showed in this chapter, a high degree of freedom can be reached by avoiding the chains of a fixed residence and by changing your attitudes. These, combined with knowledge, can give you the freedom, health, and security that only the richest men in the world could hope to emulate.

RVs the Key to Freedom

"The world is a book, and those who do not travel, read only a page."

— **St. Augustine**

Nearly every time I watch the news I see people complain about wages, housing, prices, taxes, regulation, *ad nauseam*. It seems that the ills of the world are pressing around the citizens of the United States and the only solution is to surrender our lives to the government in hopes that the bureaucrats will toss us the crumbs that will make life tolerable.

I have mixed feelings when I see the mentality of many Americans. I despair because our country is becoming more authoritarian and is headed down that slippery slope that has dragged other nations to revolution. On the other hand, the situation is humorous because an answer is within their reach and they only have to take their blinders off and see the other opportunities to solve these problems.

The solution I found was the Recreational Vehicle (RV). It let me avoid the fixed residence that causes so many of our problems and it changed my perception of life.

You can buy "live-in" RVs for less than $5,000 (1990 prices). They give you all the comforts of a regular house, but in a compact package that can go nearly anywhere. You can live in a god-forsaken spot and still enjoy hot water, refrigerator, heat, air conditioning, microwave, TV, VCR, etc. I even know people who have installed copiers, telephones, faxes, and satellite dishes on their RVs. The search for freedom doesn't require hardship and sacrifice. If you want to emulate Gandhi, go ahead, but it isn't necessary. You can achieve a great deal of freedom just by moving into an RV.

You Can Shop for Less Government

Although the federal government restricts our lives with a plethora of useless regulations, most laws are still found at the state or local level. That means the nearly endless mixture of freedom and regulation found at the local level represents a buffet for the RV owner to sample. You can move until you find the ideal spot for you or you can use each spot for your own needs (make major purchases in states without sales tax, residency in states without state income tax, and car registration elsewhere). Obviously, politicians get upset when people move in order to avoid regulation and sometimes try to insist you become a resident of their state. Just remember, this is a free country and there isn't a law that makes you the property of a given state. Serfdom has been abolished and you can move anywhere you want.

Since politicians have a fixation on stationary citizens, they often pass laws in the foolish belief that people would rather obey their silly regulations than move. An RV lifestyle changes that. Anytime a community restricts your freedom, you have the freedom to leave and let the politicians regulate each other.

Become an Invisible Citizen

When the 1990 census was made, no one counted me. I didn't receive a form and nobody came to my RV to count the number of residents. At the same time bureaucrats and social workers were racking their brains in order to count the uncounted (usually to obtain more taxpayer dollars), they were ignoring a part of the population that surely outnumbers the residents of steam grates.

The reason for the oversight again revolves around the bureaucrats' vision of respectable, employed people living in houses and the rest living on a steam grate. If you don't live in a house and you choose not to advertise yourself by registering to vote, you won't show up on those numerous lists that the government keeps to track their citizens, send out tax bills, summon to jury duty, and generally harass. If you use the philosophy that the government can only limit your freedom if they know you exist and know where you are, invisibility is the surest route to freedom.

Guerrilla Freedom: A Fish in the Ocean

Mao compared a guerrilla with a fish living in the ocean of the population. Someone living the "Freedom Road" lifestyle is a guerrilla; denying the government his support and letting others know that freedom is available to all. Like the guerrilla fighter, you can slip into the general population and appear to be a conventional citizen. After all, you have a normal RV like millions of other regular citizens, you can dress normally when you are with other people, and you don't need to yell, "Off the pigs," to passing patrol cars. How are they to know that you are a menace to the state? To catch you they would have to check out every other "normal" citizen. And, if they did check out each citizen, they would just create more enemies.

RVs Imply Respectability

Every year hundreds of thousands of respectable retired people head south for the winter. Each summer millions take their RVs out to visit each part of the country. When residents and police see these RVs, they immediately imagine either a retired couple enjoying a quiet retirement or a diligent working family taking two weeks off before returning to the conventional hard-working, tax-paying life. In addition, since RVs mean tourist dollars, most governments are a little more lenient toward RV occupants since they don't want to earn a bad reputation and lose business and the resultant tax dollars.

RV Life is Inexpensive

How much money would you need if you didn't have a mortgage, a job (which means spending on clothes, a car, expensive vacation, and that favorite excuse, "I deserve it. I worked hard all week."), most utilities, cable TV, a place to put all the things you buy, and neighbors to keep up with. Now imagine how little you would need to work to pay for the rest of your monetary needs. Sounds attractive, doesn't it? You could either work part time and have more leisure time or you could take a low paying job you like.

Paying cash for an RV immediately relieves you of the heavy mortgage (or rent) and property taxes most Americans live under. And since RVs are smaller and designed to operate independently, they require less utilities and power than a conventional house. That means less monthly costs and less environmental impact.

RVs also have other benefits. They are smaller, so you think twice before you buy something. You are also less likely to have a telephone or cable TV to spend money on. Finally, you can park your home where the taxes are the lowest.

Living in a recreational vehicle doesn't guarantee less spending, but it takes an undying dedication to the materialistic lifestyle to spend all that money.

Freedom from Wealth

Modern life is a jungle for the rich. The current concept of tort law is to sue the person with the most money, not the guilty party (if there is one). People with less money are rarely the targets of a suit or a sales pitch by salesmen.

Poverty also protects you from the biggest oppressor, the government. Centuries ago, when the king needed money, he would accuse a duke or prince of some imaginary crime. He would then confiscate the victim's property and sell it to someone else for cash. This was one reason the lords wanted King John to sign the Magna Charta: to require due process and a jury of their peers before confiscation.

Today, the money-hungry government targets rich individuals and companies and seizes assets before a trial. Not only is it easier than waiting for the effort of a trial, but it often forces the destitute victim to plead guilty to a lesser crime (and a hefty penalty) in order to retain part of their assets. King John would have approved.

The low cost lifestyle of an RV eliminates harassment from those who want your wealth. It also gives you a public relations advantage. Americans love an underdog and lend a sympathetic ear to stories of the "mistreated" poor. What lawyer or prosecutor would want to tell a jury that he is trying to stick it to a poor person?

Hinder Government

If you want a smaller government, do you think your one vote will change anything? Not as long as you pay your taxes and politicians can use your money to buy a dozen other votes. Of course, you could refuse to pay taxes, but that's risky. The legal way is to stop paying your taxes by not making enough money to tax. That is a potent weapon that can put a dent in any government.

For example, imagine an educated middle class couple that makes $40,000 each. Their total household income is $80,000 and the average tax burden is $35,000. If they bought an RV and started living a cheaper lifestyle, they could live well on $8,000. The taxes on $8,000 are minimal and they have taken $35,000 from the government. That means the government must borrow the money (and they can't borrow it from you), raise taxes (and upset more voters), or cut services (less bureaucrats and less votes they can buy). The couple that drops out can do more to create small government than they could ever accomplish with their votes. Imagine what would happen if 100,000 did this!

Choose Your Neighbors

Remember the neighbor who didn't like your lawn? In a house you have to put up with him and hope he doesn't call the lawn police. With RVs, you or your neighbor could leave (it just depends on who wants to leave more).

Summary

"Who dares nothing, need hope for nothing."

— **Johann von Schiller**

In modern America, freedom exists only in civics classes and political speeches. The freedom and individuality that our forefathers fought for has been reduced to a few token rights. If we sit idly by, those lost freedoms will never be regained. We can start by rejecting the conventional life and living in a manner that allows us to enjoy freedom while denying the government the money and support necessary to continue this tyranny. At the least, we regain our own freedom; at best, we help a nation regain its freedom.

3

Preparing For Freedom

"To be a grain of sand in the engine of government, you must break yourself off the rock of society."

— **Harold Hough**

The road to freedom requires a first step: eliminating your dependence on society. Some of that's mental, realizing that society has nothing as valuable as your freedom. The rest takes hard work and maybe years of planning.

Many of you are thinking, "RVs are a great way to live and achieve more freedom, but I'm so loaded down with debt that I can't think about leaving my job or buying a trailer. I have a mortgage, car payments, credit cards, and other bills. I'm already behind in some of my payments. If the phone isn't ringing off the hook with bill collectors, it's probably been disconnected. I can't get out of debt."

You're wrong. Paying all your debts is easier than you think. Why? Because I had the same problems. But I eliminated my debt in two years, started a serious savings program and in less than five years after my problems I was living the ideal life on the road.

The American Nightmare

"A man in debt so far is a slave."

— **Ralph Waldo Emerson**

The American Dream sure has changed. Once Americans were rugged individualists, carving a nation out of the wilderness. Today individualism is out and herd instincts are in. No one wants to stand by themselves. Now everyone wants to be part of the "in" crowd.

Materialism and spending are part of any group you want to belong to. The establishment buys expensive gadgets, fine homes, popular cars, the latest fashions, and expensive vacations. The mark of a successful person is the possessions they own. If they own the right combination of goods, they are immediately judged successful. Of course, that leads many "unsuccessful" people to spend or borrow money to emulate the rich, but that doesn't bother the merchants or bankers.

Even the anti-establishment groups have their materialistic requirements. The environmental groups want you to spend money for recycled paper, adopting a whale, to decry capitalism while advocating more state interference, and to give more money to environmental groups so they can hire lawyers that add to the maze of laws. They may decry our materialistic society, but they're the first to try to benefit from it.

No matter what group you belong to, the government doesn't mind. Your consumption is the prime component of their measure of economic success. If you don't spend enough, they start to worry (of course, if they need more taxes, they say you're spending too much). Your spending also forces you to earn more money to pay taxes. If you didn't buy, you wouldn't need as much money and you wouldn't pay enough taxes to keep the politicians happy. That's why in 1990 the Secretary of Health and Human Services, Samuel Skinner, complained about the prevalence of smoking. He accused smoking of causing illness that robbed the national economy of millions of man days of work. He implied that illness without sufficient cause is economic sabotage and a crime against the United States. Those familiar with history know that Nazis and Communists used the crime of economic sabotage to eliminate their opponents.

Another reason the government prefers materialistic citizens is the ease with which you can control them. As the communists found out when their citizens rebelled in 1989 and 1990, you can't control the mind. You can only control material possessions and when people don't have any worldly goods, you lose any hold over them.

The United States has mastered the art of material control. If you do the right things, you'll be rewarded with government money or tax breaks so you can continue to accumulate goods. If you interfere with the government, they will confiscate your goods and leave you without your expensive house and compact disc player. Only people with money could be controlled that way.

Materialism also makes us easier to find. One reason many Jews refused to leave Nazi Germany was that they would be forced to leave their possessions behind. As a result, their own wealth condemned them to death.

Today, with our reliance on credit we are even easier to find. What the police don't know, our credit card companies can find out. We willingly sold our privacy for thirty pieces of silver; to borrow money we told credit companies things we would never tell the government. Little did we realize when we filled out those credit applications, the government can gain access to those records whenever they want.

So the Great American Dream is now the Great American Nightmare. Our quest for material goods has condemned us to our current jobs, striped us of our individuality, made us obey government edicts, made us provide more taxes for the government, and made it easier for the government to track us. If someone tried to pass laws giving government this power, we would lynch him. Instead we have sacrificed ourselves for the transient pleasure of a few goods. Even if you never decide to live the Freedom Road lifestyle, this first step will improve your life. If you can't take it, you will never be free of the government.

Escaping the Trap

"Everyone thinks of changing the world, but no one thinks of changing himself."

— **Leo Tolstoy**

Realizing the problems materialism creates for ourselves and our freedom is the first and most important goal in a better lifestyle. The second goal is to regain your self esteem.

Ever since we were in school, individuality has been suppressed. We are forced to conform and act as part of a group. That, in part, is the problem with our materialistic world. Since we must belong to a group we must buy the badges of membership. That forces us to purchase expensive cars and big houses as well as the latest fad.

But, if we have a high degree of self esteem and prize our individuality, we have little reason to buy objects that don't meet our needs. A person without pride is more likely to spend money in order to belong to a socially acceptable crowd than someone who is content with his accomplishments and doesn't seek public acceptance.

Regaining your self esteem isn't hard. If you agree freedom is more important than all the goods that can be offered, you have already set yourself off from the crowd. You are questioning the value of government and the standards of society. Be proud of your differences. Don't worry what others, including your boss, think. Remember, in a few years you will be living a lifestyle that they envy, but aren't smart enough to follow.

The largest obstacle that separates you from the Freedom Road lifestyle is debt. I can't make paying your bills any more attractive, but I can provide a few suggestions to make it easier. If you need more help, visit a library or buy a book on managing your money. It will give you more suggestions.

To eliminate debt, you must stop using it. That means cutting up the credit cards and sending them back to the company. Don't keep them because you want them for an emergency or business travel. Your emergencies will be covered out of savings from now on. As far as business travel goes, your company should give you an advance and rental car credit card prior to any trip.

Many companies want you to travel on your credit card because they're receiving an interest free loan on your credit. But a company that wants you to travel should expect to foot the bill. Just tell them you don't believe in credit cards and you can't travel unless they finance the trip. If they value you and want you to travel, they will find a solution. If they really want the free loan from your card, they will pressure you by saying credit cards are necessary for a successful businessman. However, after ten years in the business world, I never found a situation that required my own credit card.

While many people will belittle your lack of credit, many will give you grudging praise for your self control. In fact, most people will act like you lost 50 pounds on a diet and ask you how you had the self control to do it. By using your self esteem, you just turned a bad situation into a positive event. You let others know you don't need credit and you can handle any problem yourself.

Of course, credit cards also provide identification, but remember there isn't a law that requires possession of a credit card or requires one for identification. Just use your self esteem to pull you through. Once, while opening a bank account, the bank officer told us that we needed to identify ourselves with one picture ID and two credit cards. Many people would have blushed and mumbled they didn't have credit cards (and implied they were unreliable). I took a different tack.

"Madam, I don't believe in credit cards. I pay everything in cash. If I had credit cards, I wouldn't have this amount of money to deposit in your bank."

"But, we need to know your credit worthiness so we can issue a Mastercard and a check cashing card to you."

"I don't want a credit card. I've done well enough without them."

"But, you still need a check cashing card so you can cash checks at the grocery store."

"I always pay cash at the grocery store."

"But, you really need one."

"Why?"

When we left we had our account even though we didn't have credit cards. We even received our check cashing cards, although we haven't used them yet. The moral of the story is that you don't need credit cards for identification. Just tell people you're too smart to borrow money. Few people can argue with that.

Without plastic, the problem of debt diminishes. Most individuals only have mortgages and car loans after consumer debt. But, both can be reduced or even eliminated with planning and self esteem.

Housing is a racket foisted on us by builders, real estate agents, and the government. The government has added so many regulations that the average house costs an extra $15,000 to meet government standards. Builders and real estate agents have convinced us that houses are an investment. Personally, I consider anything that needs mowing, repairs, cleaning, and costs money to maintain a lousy investment. Most of the increased value of a house is caused by inflation or the cost of regulation in new homes.

You've read enough of this book to know my solution to the high cost of housing is the recreational vehicle. Probably the money you spend for mortgage payments in one year will buy a nice RV. The sooner you move out of your house or apartment and into an RV, the sooner you cut your debt.

Cars are a necessity, but they are also the biggest status symbol. We buy luxury cars to show we're rich, we buy sports cars to show we have style, we even buy expensive "economy" cars to display our thrift. Are we buying these cars because we need them or because we need to make a status statement? If we have a high level of self esteem, we don't mind driving a clunker.

That's not to say we can't enjoy our cars. I personally enjoy a nimble sports car. But instead of dropping a fortune on a big name car that would send teenage girls into rapture, I bought a used Alfa Romeo sedan for the price of the monthly payment of an expensive car. It doesn't look as sharp, but its performance is equal to cars that cost 50 times as much. True, I don't attract attention from the admiring public, but I also avoid the attention of the police.

Saving

"If debt is a shackle then saving is the key. But, having more than one key is a burden and unnecessary."

— **Harold Hough**

Earlier, I said that savings are a bond to our current lifestyle. That's true. However, we do need some money to start on our new life. The amount you choose to save depends on your needs. You may already have enough saved or you may need to save for a couple of years.

You should save money for three things: an RV, to develop income potential, and emergencies. A recreational vehicle will be the biggest expenditure, depending on how sophisticated you want to be. You will also probably need to invest in something to provide you with an income, unless you already have a mobile skill. Finally, you need some money for emergencies on the road and something to ease you out of the traditional lifestyle and into the mobile one.

The first rule of saving is to take your savings out of your paycheck as soon as possible; preferably with a savings program at work. The reason is easy: if you don't see it, you don't miss it and you learn to live without it. Don't worry about your current financial situation, you should always set at least a little aside.

The other easy way to save is to increase your savings every time you receive a pay raise or you finish an installment loan. You maintain your standard of living while putting aside the money needed for your new life.

Learn Simple and Inexpensive Pleasures

"Most of the luxuries and many of the comforts of life are not only dispensable, but positive hindrances to the elevation of mankind."
— **Henry David Thoreau**

A friend was once bemoaning the decline in manufacturing in the United States. There was nothing more indicative that we were dying as a nation, he said than our evolution to a service economy. I reminded him that goods are merely tools. We are not interested in the materials, but the services they provide. For instance, automobiles provide transportation, but if a device could instantly move us from one place to another, the demand for autos would decline dramatically.

Sometimes we fail to realize in our modern world, that we really only want services, not goods, to make our lives happier and better. Sometimes in our rush to buy something, we fail to realize that we can achieve the same satisfaction for less money.

Anyone who wants to divorce themselves from society must learn how to become happier without money. I can't tell you exactly how to do it because I don't know what makes you happy and what substitutes are acceptable. However, I can tell you how my wife and I lowered our costs of entertainment.

Back when I worked a conventional job, we would spend Saturday eating out and catching a movie or a baseball game. It was an enjoyable way to spend a day, but it cost over a hundred dollars a week. That was a big hunk of money to spend just to unwind from a week of work.

What we really wanted was a change of pace, a nice meal we could sit back and enjoy, and some entertainment. When we started living on the road, we found some inexpensive solutions. For instance, if we're staying in one area for awhile, we buy a one year pass to a local attraction. These passes usually cost no more than two trips to the site and they can be used as often as we want. At the same time, since we see the place more often, we can take our time and enjoy ourselves instead of rushing. We also visit free attractions like an old local church, library, or a museum. We even spent one day with friends looking at scrapped military aircraft through the fence. A new experience doesn't have to cost money — you can have just as much fun by enjoying free attractions.

We also satisfied our needs for a relaxing meal and entertainment at home. On Sunday I cook up one of our favorite "luxury" meals like smoked salmon, fresh vegetables, and champagne. Then we pick a video tape to watch (we've owned a VCR for ten years and have a large library of movies recorded from TV), set up the meal, and enjoy a good movie with a repast fit for a king. Best of all, this costs less than a meal at a fast food restaurant (fortunately, my wife prefers cheap champagne). After an afternoon. of luxurious living, we feel just as if we had visited the best restaurant and gone to the theater. Our spirits are refreshed and our wallet is still whole.

This concept can be applied to any pleasure. There is an old story of an executive who spent his two week vacation at the same Canadian lake each year. Each year he had the same guide who always managed to show him the best places to fish. After many years the executive asked him how much he made. The guide told him and the executive was shocked at how little it was.

"Look, I know you are a good worker. I'll hire you for four times what you are making here if you come to work for me at my company."

The guide shook his head and refused.

"Why not? Don't you want to make more money?"

"Let me ask you one thing. With all the money you make, what is the most expensive enjoyable thing you can spend it on?"

"This fishing trip is the best thing," was the reply.

"Well, you see, I don't need the money, I've already got that."

If you know what makes you happy, you can find an inexpensive alternative. Just use your imagination and don't consider money as the only solution. Remember, your mind is the most important tool for happiness.

Cut Costs

"There's always an alternative."

— **Anonymous**

Creativity is a tool for enjoying ourselves, but it can also be a tool for finding alternatives and lowering costs. If you applied self esteem to your buying habits and are still having problems saving money, eliminating debt, and paying your bills, there are still other possibilities. Conventional wisdom tells you to see a credit counselor (and spend some money) or go into bankruptcy (and spend more money). There is an easier solution: find a job where you make less money.

People talk about the different cost of living in different areas of the country, but few think about it. However, the difference is so great you can take a lower paying job elsewhere and save. In our case, we moved from a suburb of Washington, DC to a city near Pittsburgh, Pennsylvania even though our family income dropped about $10,000.

Near Pittsburgh we found nice housing for a fraction of Washington prices. Houses near closed steel mills were selling for as little as $6,000 and 30 acre farms with stone houses cost $7,000. Our housing bill went from $550 (rent) to $180 (mortgage, insurance, and property tax). We were even living in a lower crime area.

The savings from housing, taxes, food, and transportation actually exceeded the lost income and we were able to pay our debts and save money. This move taught me two things. The first was there is always a creative solution to any problem. The other lesson was that money isn't always the solution to everything.

Making a Timetable

"Adventure is not outside a man; it is within."

— David Grayson

The first part of this chapter talked about the problems of the American Dream and the tools needed to escape it. They are, however, worthless if you don't act decisively. You must decide to move and develop a timetable to act.

There isn't a fixed time to move from your current condition to freedom. It all depends on your desire, your level of debt, the amount of money you save, and your prospects for making money on the road. If everything is working well, you could leave in months. However, you should plan at least six months; more if you need money and have some debt. It took five years for me to eliminate a staggering debt, save enough money, and become a paid writer.

Your desire to be free is the most important factor. If you're willing to sacrifice current pleasures and are willing to have limited material needs in the future, you can join the Freedom Road quickly. The wisest choice is to pick a pace you can manage without quitting.

Debt will be the largest factor in the time it takes to achieve your freedom. Most credit card debt is calculated to liquidate itself (if you stop spending) in two years. Many car loans, however, last much longer. If you're the typical consumer and loaded with debt, it might be wise to set your timetable around two years. That allows you to pay the credit card debt at the minimum while using the extra money to pay the longer auto debts and save money. This isn't the wisest choice in terms of the interest spent, but it's easy. If you stick to this plan, you should be ready to move as soon as your last credit card bill is paid.

Most Americans are poor savers. If you're the typical American, your savings account is probably small. Therefore, you need to save enough for an RV, about 6 months living expenses, and some emergency cash. When you finish reading this book, decide on the type of RV you want and how much you should spend. Then establish a monthly budget when you travel. Calculate how much money you should have in reserve and what you want for an emergency. Then, accounting for your debt payments and required cash, you can determine how long it will take for you to go on the road.

Having a job that you can travel with won't put you on the road quicker, but it can cut down on what you need to save. As a rule, the more mobile your job, the less you have to save.

Having evaluated these four factors, use your debt and savings situation to develop a schedule that leaves you with enough money and no debt (assume you sell your house to eliminate your mortgage). With this as a preliminary timetable, decide what your new profession will be and determine if you can become proficient in that time. If you can, ask yourself if you are happy with the schedule. Do you need more time or do you want to break free earlier? If so, decide what sacrifices you're willing to make and adjust the date accordingly.

Once you establish a time frame, set a date to leave in your RV. Then fill in the rest of your schedule with important dates like selling your house, paying debts, quitting work, buying your RV, and other critical milestones. Then stick to the schedule, review dates, and update them as necessary. If you plan it properly, you shouldn't have any problems leaving when you planned.

Learn Survival Skills

"Simplicity is making the journey of this life with just baggage enough."

— **Charles Warner**

Our pioneer forefathers made their own clothes, food and homes. That ability was critical to their freedom because it limited their reliance on others. Today, however, we're all specialists and depend on each other to live. For instance, how many times have you heard someone complain about their authorized auto mechanic, yet they still patronize him? Why? Because they're unable to make their own repairs so they must compromise their principles to deal with someone they would rather avoid.

Interdependence is great for someone who wants to be a part of society, but someone who wants independence and earns less money must learn to do many things for himself. Fortunately, most of the things we require "experts" for are really simple and can even be fun to learn.

Once as a disbursing officer in the Navy I had a safe mechanism fail (when the door was open) while out on the Mediterranean. Rather than deal with the hassle of shifting the money around and finding a government authorized repairman, I opened the mechanism and looked at it myself, even though I knew nothing about combination locks. Within half an hour I found out how the mechanism worked, discovered one part that was too worn to operate, and stuck a piece of tape on it to compensate for the worn metal. When I left two years later, it was still working. Not only had I saved the government money, but I had an opportunity to learn about combination locks.

A self sufficient life has many opportunities for learning, but you have to be willing to tackle them. Between now and the time you leave, force yourself to become more self reliant. For instance, instead of taking your car to a mechanic to change the oil, learn to do it yourself. It gives you an opportunity to learn about the engine compartment in addition to saving money. You should also take the time to learn more about car repair (if your car is one of the new "black box" types, think about trading it in for a older car you can work on).

Another important part of self sufficiency is learning what's important. When we have money in our pocket, we tend to want to do everything. When we do the work ourselves, we learn what we can and can't live with. For instance you may have a water pump that leaks in your RV whenever you use it. However, if you only use it on the road because you stay in RV parks most of the time, it may be wise to delay the repair until you really need it.

Procrastination is also another tool of the self sufficient person. If you delay the task, you may discover that you really don't need to repair or replace some items. At worst, you're delaying investing time and money into the problem. For instance, a few years ago someone riding in my car noticed a noise in my rear wheel bearing. When I called my mechanic, he told me the design of the bearing was such that the wheel would continue to work indefinitely, although the noise would become worse. He suggested I worry about it when I brought the car in for some other work. A year later I finally brought the car in and he replaced the part. Although I had been harassed by my friends in the previous year (when are you going to get that fixed), the time value of the money saved was twenty dollars. Additionally, I could fit the repair into my budget so there weren't any surprises.

If you want freedom from a regular job while traveling the open road, you must become self sufficient. That includes knowing what needs to be done, knowing when it needs to be done, and then being able to do it. Start developing your skills as soon as you can and by the time you leave, you will be surprised at what you can do and what you have learned.

Job Skills

"Make yourself necessary to somebody."
— **Ralph Waldo Emerson**

Sometime, while preparing for your freedom, you must decide on a new profession. Then you have to dedicate the time to mastering your new skills.

Some readers will be lucky enough to have an occupation that easily fits RV life. For instance, construction people, willing to move around the country, are always in demand. They can follow the money and then use the high wages to relax the rest of the time.

The rest of us probably have to find a new profession. While a later chapter deals with different occupations, I want to discuss some factors that may help you select an enjoyable and profitable profession.

Most of us have romantic dreams of becoming a famous writer, artist, or photographer. We will travel around the country, drawing on our experiences to make masterpieces. While we're enriching the arts our publishers and clients will be enriching us with multi-million dollar deals.

If that's your dream, you better be prepared for a hard landing at an alternate airport. Writing, painting, and photography are glamorous fields and the competition is stiff. If you do break into one of these fields, you will need to work hard for small pay. However, with the inexpensive lifestyle of Freedom Road, you can realistically compete with others.

I do not want to belittle your dreams. They are, in fact, the most important part of your future life, because the whole concept behind Freedom Road is to do what you like. But, like everything, they must be tempered with an analysis of your skills, the tools you have, and the amount of money you need.

Your first step is to ask yourself what you want to do for a living. Then look at this dream profession and ask yourself if you really have the skills and if you want to pursue it full-time. If, for instance, you want to write, you must be able to tell yourself honestly that you have the skills to communicate and you must be willing to dedicate 40 hours a week to it.

First, practice your new profession a little bit. If you want to be a writer, spend your weekends writing for the newsletter of an organization you belong to. If you want to be a photographer, maybe the newsletter can use photos; or if an artist, do some sketches. Then after a month, ask if you really enjoyed working 8 hours on a Saturday, if your work was good enough not to embarrass the paper, and if you met the deadline (no excuses). If you said no to any of these questions, you probably should think about a different profession, or keep at it until you can say "yes" to all of them.

If your dream doesn't seem to offer you a living, don't give up hope. With the free time offered by this lifestyle you can still pursue your goal and maybe with enough hard work you will finally be able to make some money at it. Until then, you need to find something else to earn the money you need.

Your next step is to assess your skills and tools and try to fit them into a freer lifestyle. For instance, if you were good at making presentations at your job, maybe you can become an after dinner speaker at gatherings. Or, if you have an unused printing press in the basement, you can produce advertising or small newsletters. There are many niches you can fill and you are only limited by your imagination.

After you settle on a future profession, be sure it fits into your future lifestyle. Will you be able to make enough money to live? Does the job require more or less travel than you plan? Can you enjoy remote, idyllic scenery while still earning enough money? Make sure it fits before you go further.

Sometimes the job isn't as perfect as you thought. Before I left on the road, one of the writing jobs I had arranged required travelling and reporting on one type of event across the United States. The pay wasn't high, but it was a regular check and would pay for gasoline as we crossed the country. Everything went well for the first six months, until it became clear I would have to travel out of my planned path to cover new places. That made the cost higher than it was worth.

This seemingly ideal assignment had become a problem because it required more travel than I had planned. Fortunately, I came up with a solution. I called friends and asked them to cover local shows for money. I then took their notes and turned them into articles. The column survived although I had to share some of the money.

So carefully analyze your job plans before you leave. If you don't, you'll have to make adjustments on the road. That will force you to dip into your savings and may make a carefree trip miserable.

Summary

"Even if you are on the right track — you'll get run over if you just sit there."

— **Arthur Godfrey**

This has been the most important chapter. Earlier we discussed how we can achieve freedom on the road. Later, we discuss the finer points of this lifestyle. But this is all worthless if you don't take the first steps to cut the cords to society and move on to a better style of life.

If you want to achieve more freedom, you must act. Your first step is to eliminate those habits like debt, spending, and expensive tastes that you gained from our materialistic society. Then, develop a timetable to leave your present life and strike out on your own. Finally, learn those skills that allow you to be self sufficient and able to earn money on the move.

To start you on the road, set a date for your new life and write it down on paper. Now under it write those factors that may affect that time (debt, savings, and job prospects). As you read this book, make other notes that have an impact on that date. When you complete the book, look at those factors and see if your original date should be changed. Once you have set a date, make a timetable with important milestones like selling your house and buying an RV. Then, if you really want your freedom and you stick to that schedule, there will come a time when you close the door to your old house for the last time, start up the engine, and head down the road that holds your freedom.

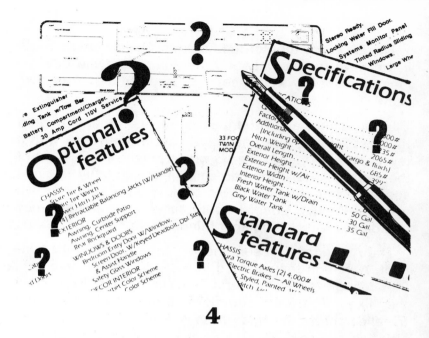

4

Choosing The Right RV

"We are a rebellious nation. Our whole history is treason; our blood was attained before we were born; our creeds were infidelity to the mother church; our constitution treason to our fatherland."

— Theodore Parker

Independence requires a tool. The American colonists used guns as their tool to gain freedom. In fact, the first battle of Lexington and Concord was an attempt by British soldiers to confiscate an arsenal of muskets owned by radicals (a fact conveniently forgotten by gun control advocates). With guns, they had the power to force the British out of the Colonies.

The RV is the tool for the Freedom Road lifestyle. With it, we have the mobility and invisibility to avoid government and society while keeping those civilized things we want.

In the Sixties and Seventies, some libertarians thought the best lifestyle was one carved out of the forest with a few handtools and sheltered with a plastic sheet. Most of them couldn't take the hardships and inevitably rejoined society. Even Thoreau moved back into the city after two years at Walden Pond. In both cases they thought they could exist without the finer things in life.

The American pioneers, however, had a different concept. Although they wanted independence and freedom, they recognized that civilization gave them some luxuries they liked. There are countless stories of pioneers who travelled across the wilderness with musical instruments, libraries, or fine china. These compromises allowed them to face the hardships of the wilderness without regretting their choice.

We want the same thing. We want a life removed from the oppression of government and society while giving us some comforts that make life better. That's why an RV is the perfect answer. It gives you the mobility you want while offering most of the comforts of your present home.

Any RV you intend to buy should meet three criteria for comfort and freedom. They are:

Comfort

Your RV should be comfortable enough to make you forget about living in a house. Many freedom seekers feel a small truck camper or van can provide cheap, mobile living. Unfortunately, after a few months living cheek to jowl with their partner, not having hot showers, and not having any luxuries, they give up. These may be nice for weekend trips, but most people need more space and some privacy over long periods of time. When you choose your RV, be sure it's large enough to feel comfortable. Before you buy it, spend about half an hour (without a salesman or owner) moving about in it and sitting or lying down.

We spent about six months looking for a perfect RV, and our hunt was successful. Our current motorhome is preferable to our old house because it's more comfortable and airy. If you make the same effort, you should find a new home that makes you forget your old house.

Mobility

In order to remain invisible, your RV should be mobile. As we discussed in the second chapter, the government expects people to live at fixed residences in normal communities. They find it hard to deal with people who move or live in the wilderness. Therefore, your RV should be able to move and you should avoid any second hand bargains that have major mechanical flaws. But, more important, your home should be small enough to travel unpaved roads into national wilderness. That eliminates some of the monstrous motorhomes seen at some RV parks. These rigs are only good for prepared sites and they can't be used in the wilderness.

In some ways, mobility conflicts with comfort because the smaller the rig, the more places it can go. Therefore, you have to make a decision about how much comfort you want and how much mobility you require. A rig smaller than 30 feet should be able to go anywhere but the roughest parts of the mountains with few problems because most unpaved roads are designed to handle large trucks. At the same time, an RV that size should have all the comforts you want. If on the other hand, you want to live where you can't be found, you'll have to sacrifice comfort for the ability to go anywhere. However, unless you have a serious problem with seeing other people, you can achieve a great deal of privacy for less trouble.

Self Sufficiency

Self sufficiency is important to anyone seeking freedom because our dependence often forces us to compromise our principles. We tolerate the power company, despite their arrogant attitude, because we need electricity. We even act nice to petty government officials, because they dole out the tax money. We fear a collapse of society because the disruptions may make our life inconvenient. A well chosen RV will free you from these concerns.

After water, power is the most important concern. Most RVs, even the smallest, have propane tanks. These can power the stove, furnace, refrigerator, and sometimes even the lights. A good RV should have a propane tank large enough to keep you running for two to four weeks without refilling. If you need more, you can buy additional propane bottles.

Electricity is provided in a RV by two sources: the auxiliary batteries and an optional generator. RVs have a separate battery that runs lights and any 12 volt electrical requirements so the motor battery doesn't discharge. These batteries are usually "deep discharge" batteries that provide more power than a conventional auto battery. When the engine is running, the alternator charges them in addition to the auto battery.

Battery systems are great for weekend trips, but you need more power for true independence (unless you use little electricity). You should also have a generator to recharge the system and occasionally provide regular household current. Although the cost per kilowatt hour is 5 to 10 times as much as you would pay through the power system, you'll find that you don't use as much electricity and will probably spend less than you would at home.

If you choose a self-sufficient RV, you'll find life in the wildest parts of America to be just as comfortable as life in the poshest suburbs. You also have the added comfort of knowing that whatever happens to the power company or the government, you'll stay safe and comfortable.

Recreational Vehicle Styles

"He who chooses the beginning of a road chooses the place it leads to."

— **Harry Emerson Fosdick**

If you choose the wrong RV, you'll probably give up the Freedom Road lifestyle in less than a year. Therefore, you should take your time and consider all the alternatives. If you established a timetable in the last chapter, you should give yourself at least six months to shop for your new home. If your schedule is longer because of debts or savings, go ahead and start looking today because the longer you look, the better your choice. The additional time also gives you the opportunity to think about your new life and may inspire you to keep paying your debts.

My wife and I spent two years looking at RVs before we bought the one we wanted. During that time we went to dealers and looked at the classified ads. We even spent time looking at expensive models because they gave us a better idea of what conveniences were available for a Freedom Road lifestyle. When the time came to buy one, we knew exactly what we wanted and we made a good deal. The two year search was worth it and we even had many enjoyable daydreams while sitting in some of these motor homes.

Motor Homes

Unless you already own a truck or car with a large engine designed for towing, you might want to look at motor homes first. Although they cost more than a travel trailer, they are cheaper to operate than a trailer and a vehicle suitable for towing.

There are three classes of motor homes: Classes A, B, and C. Class A is the one we are most familiar with. They are conversions of truck or bus chassis and range from about 20 feet to 40 feet long. They are spacious homes and are a luxurious way to travel long distances.

Class B motor homes are popularly called van conversions. They offer an everyday vehicle with the ability to be used as a camper on the weekend. Although they're nice for short vacations and long trips, they aren't recommended for a Freedom Road lifestyle unless you're a retired submariner and you never thought your sub quarters were crowded.

Class C motor homes are conversions of a van or pick up truck chassis. These micro motor homes have much of the convenience of the Class A models without the size or price. They have more mobility than the Class As and can be an excellent vehicle for either a single person or a couple that knows they can survive close quarters.

ADVANTAGES

1. They are excellent road machines. They are better balanced than towed rigs and have enough power, although micros may be a little sluggish on hills. Since you're higher than most other drivers (especially in the Class A), you have better visibility. The driver's seat is usually luxurious so you don't feel as stiff after a day's driving.

2. They are more maneuverable on and off roads than a towed vehicle.

3. More usable space for the size.

4. The conveniences of home are already with you. You never have to buy lunch anywhere and you can always enjoy the comforts of home while waiting for someone's doctor appointment. You can even use your own restroom instead of a public one.

5. The driving area is a usable part of the home. Usually the seats can turn around and join the living room. It can also serve as a bedroom or storage area.

6. It's easier to set up and get under way.

DISADVANTAGES

1. You have to unhook and pick up everything before traveling anywhere.

2. Gas mileage is poor, although not much worse than a vehicle with a large motor for towing.

3. If you have engine problems, you may have to pay for a hotel room.

4. They're hard to drive through small crowded streets and parking spaces can be hard to find.

Travel Trailers

If you already have a vehicle that can tow and you plan to spend less time on the road and more time set up in one place, the travel trailer may be the best option for you. Like the motor home, they come in several types, but three of the major types are the *pop-up trailer*, the *travel trailer*, and the *fifth wheel*.

The pop-up trailer is the only one that can be towed by a conventional car. It has an upper part that resembles a tent. When it's towed, the tent part is folded down into the lower part and the rig is ready for towing. Unfortunately, these have the same problems as tents. They do not retain heat and rain can leak inside. They aren't a good choice for a full-time, Freedom Road lifestyle. If, however, you find a pop-up with metal sides and you don't have many needs, it may work out.

Travel trailers are popular, especially for retired people who head south for the winter. They can be set up like a home while the towing vehicle is used as the family car. Sizes range from boxes that can be towed by most cars (but offer little space) to 30 foot models that require a pickup truck.

Fifth wheels are trailers that are attached directly to the bed of a pickup truck. Some people insist they're more stable than a regular trailer, but some can't see the difference. However, they do offer a smaller turning radius than a conventional rig although they can only be towed by a truck.

ADVANTAGES

1. You can leave the trailer in one place and use the towing vehicle for transportation.

2. If one unit breaks (like the vehicle) you don't lose the whole rig.

3. The whole trailer space is dedicated to living. None of the space is needed for the cockpit.

DISADVANTAGES

1. Trailers don't have the tight turning radius of a motor home.

2. Trailers take longer to set up and get under way.

3. You can't use the trailer while driving.

Truck Camper

You shouldn't buy a truck camper unless 1) you're alone, 2) you really want to go back into the wilds, and 3) you consider the life of a Franciscan monk too comfortable. However, they are such an inexpensive alternative to motor homes and travel trailers that they should be considered.

Truck campers are small units that are placed in the bed of a truck. Their size usually limits them to hunters and weekend campers, but there are some people who have lived in them. Some models have all the conveniences of small motor homes, with bathrooms, refrigerators, and kitchens. If your Freedom Road life doesn't include anyone else and you thought Saint Francis of Assisi was a materialistic *bon vivant*, you can't find a cheaper way to start on the road.

ADVANTAGES

1. They are very mobile. If your truck is a four wheel drive, you can live as far away from civilization as you want.

2. Truck campers are the cheapest way to live a Freedom Road lifestyle.

3. You can leave your camper and use the truck for transportation.

4. Truck campers can fit in most parking places.

DISADVANTAGES

1. Space is very limited.

2. It's hard to live in a truck camper on a permanent basis.

The type of vehicle you choose for your freedom is a personal choice. There are no perfect answers. You have to weigh cost, mobility, comfort, self sufficiency, and needs. If you commit yourself to a full year of searching, you can even rent some models for a weekend or a vacation. The important thing is to not rush or try to live an uncomfortable life. I've known people who have tried to skimp on their RV and instead of living a carefree life, they end up surrendering to society in a few months or a year.

Features to Look For

"I believe that a simple and unassuming manner of life is best for every one, best for both the body and the mind."

— **Albert Einstein**

There are some features that are nearly indispensable in RVs that the freedom seeker must consider. Others are important for someone who will spend quite a bit of time away from civilization.

Generators

Most RVs have an auxiliary battery system charged by the engine's alternator. These may be good enough for a couple of days, but they will expire if you stay somewhere for more than a weekend or so. You can recharge the batteries by running the engine or you could buy a generator. The generator uses less gasoline and it also provides 110 volt AC current so you can use regular household appliances like a TV or computer.

The cost of producing your own electricity is 5 to 10 times higher than hooking up with utilities, so you should use it wisely. Fortunately, RV life makes conservation easy and you usually spend less on electricity than before.

If you're running the generator, it makes sense to use several appliances at the same time to be efficient. For instance, we will often run the TV, VCR, and the microwave at the same time.

Invertor

If you need small amounts of 110 volt AC (to run small appliances), you may want an invertor. This solid state device changes 12 volt DC to 110 volt AC so you don't need to run the generator needlessly. Be aware that many types of electronics can't run on cheaper invertors, so investigate this first.

Water and Disposal

When I've been out in the wilderness, the first commodity to disappear is water. Because water is heavy and bulky to carry, most RVs have small water tanks. That means you will have to either conserve, bring more in plastic containers, or find a place to replenish your supply if you plan an extended trip into the outback. Figure at least 3 gallons per person per day unless it's hot, then bring at least 5 gallons or more. I always carry collapsible plastic water jugs if I need more.

The size of your waste disposal system is based on the size of your fresh water tank. If you pack extra fresh water, you will likely overflow your waste storage unless you plan for this. By using the great outdoors for your bathroom, you will reduce the amount of waste you have to store and how frequently you have to dump.

Propane

Propane gas is the life blood of the modern RV. It operates the refrigerator, stove, furnace, and oven. As with the water tank, you want the largest propane tank available. The best system is a pair of portable propane tanks — not an installed tank. These can be taken by car or by hand to the nearest filling station when they're empty. You can even buy more tanks if you need to stay away for awhile. With an internal system, you must bring the RV to the station or build a fitting that allows you to use portable tanks.

Storage Space

Your new home should have loads of storage space because you will need all you have. Storage pods on top of the RV are especially useful although they may make the vehicle a little top heavy. You can offset the higher center of balance by storing your books in boxes on the floor. When you stop, you can move the books to another place like the tow vehicle or the cockpit.

Awning

RVs can be small places and you may not have enough space. If you have an awning, you can spend time outside. You can use the area under the awning as a storage area or even a living room. The extra room is particularly useful if people are starting to wear on each other's nerves.

Floor Plan

When you first look at RVs, select the floor plan you want. If there are two of you, there should be two rooms so you can stay out of each other's hair. If your sleep habits are different, establish a place the one person can work or read without disturbing the other. There are many different types of floor plans, so try to find one you like.

Refrigerator

I've heard many people question the need for a refrigerator, but I have to disagree for two reasons. The first reason is that most healthy foods don't have preservatives; consequently, they spoil quickly. With a refrigerator, you can eat healthy food and not worry about chemical additives or spoilage.

The second reason is to buy food when its cheaper. With a refrigerator you can buy extra vegetables, meat, or other foodstuffs and store them. I once bought a load of green peppers and froze those I didn't use immediately. They were a delightful addition to many meals for months afterwards.

Most RV refrigerators work with both gas and electricity. Because they use so much power, the electrical setting is only useful when you're hooked to an electrical outlet. In the wilds you will use the propane. Since these units are very different from home models, you must keep them level or the coils will burn out and you will be faced with an expensive repair bill. If you park somewhere for longer than half an hour, you should either level the unit or turn it off. When you're traveling, the vibration keeps the refrigerator working properly.

Don't be lulled into buying a small refrigerator or you will be disappointed because you want the extra space. We even use ours for storing photographic film and paper.

Stove

Most RVs have them, but be sure you like the arrangement. Also check the dials and see if they give you everything between a low and a high flame. Some units don't give high heat or else give high heat and nothing else.

Water Filter

If you plan on staying in the wilderness for a long time and want to replenish your water supply with stream water, you should buy a water filter to clean the water *before putting it into the fresh water tank.* Otherwise, your water system will be contaminated and will require time consuming cleaning.

Television Antenna

I guess your need for this depends on your outlook, but I enjoy watching some TV. Since you will probably be staying in remote areas, a crank up antenna with a power signal booster for fringe area reception is necessary. Without it, you may have problems receiving some stations.

Of course, satellite dishes are now available for RVs, but they cost a lot and their power requirements are much higher.

Solar Cells

They are expensive, but if you prefer living out in the wilds for long periods, they could be worth it. They could eliminate the need for a generator (depending on your power needs) and free you from dependence on gasoline.

Good Exterior

The exterior (especially the roof) should be in good condition and free from cracks or rain damage. Check the seams on the roof for small cracks. Avoid roofs that have tar coverings — they are probably hiding something.

A good exterior also makes you invisible. A gaudy "hippiemobile" will attract police attention while a respectable RV will look like the property of an older "law abiding" retired couple or vacationer. Most communities like tourist dollars so the police generally don't hassle visitors.

Features To Avoid

RVs are part of our materialistic world, so they are often loaded with features that are of little use to the freedom seeker. Either avoid them or don't pay extra.

Air Conditioner

These things are power hogs and unless you use your generator incessantly, will force you to stay where power is available. If the location is too hot, you should move elsewhere.

Oven

Most RVs have them, but they use a lot of propane. If you already own a microwave, you probably could save money by starting the generator and using it for a few minutes rather than leaving the oven on for hours. While the generator is on, be sure to use other appliances so you don't need to run it for a long time.

Water Heater

Most RVs have them and they're useful (my wife wanted me to say that). However, you shouldn't let it run all the time. We just turn it on for showers and leave it off the rest of the time. When we need some hot water for dishes, we just heat it on the stove.

Gadgets

Many retired people sell their house and then use the money to buy an RV. That allows RV manufacturers to add expensive items that are of marginal use but add to the price. They include built-in appliances, rear viewing TV, spotlights, and other high power consumption items. In addition to their cost, they take power, occupy space, take gasoline to haul them, and break. Avoid them and stick to an inexpensive RV.

Floor Plans

There are several decisions you have to make when selecting a floor plan for your new home. Here are some of your choices:

1. Most RVs have couches in them, but their use can vary. Some couches are upholstered and convert into beds while others are plywood boxes with cushions on them. These boxes can be used for storing heavy items you want to keep low in the vehicle. If a couple of people are living in the RV, the fold out bed isn't necessary and the extra storage space may be a better way to go.

2. Eating areas in RVs are usually booths like those found in restaurants. When nighttime comes, the table is lowered and the area converts into a bed. Since it may be the only table space in the unit, you may have to decide if you want to use it as a bed or a table. Otherwise, you may have problems if one person wants to sleep and the other wants to stay up and use the table.

3. Some RVs have permanent beds that have thick mattresses. Although they're more comfortable, the space can be wasted during the day.

4. Wet baths are a combination of a shower and toilet all in one space. When the shower is used, the entire space gets wet. They take up less space, but many people don't like them.

5. Dry baths are just like the one at home. They take up more space because you have a separate toilet, tub and shower space. You can compensate for the extra space by using the bath tub for storage space when you aren't using it.

6. Some RVs have movable tables. There are holes in the floor, covered up by plugs of carpet, that hold the post for a table. You may have extra tables in a closet or you may be able to move the one table around. If you use the table for your bed, you may be able to find another one at an RV supply store.

Extra Items

There are several items you will probably have to buy or acquire with the RV. They are all readily available at a camping store.

Bubble Levels

When you park, you must keep the refrigerator level.

Toilet Chemicals

If you aren't emptying your tank and the temperature is hot, these chemicals can limit the smell. We use it very rarely, but you probably need some. Don't buy special toilet paper; regular white will break down in your sewage tank.

Sewer Hose

You need this to dump your waste water.

Water Pressure Regulator

Many places have high water pressure that can destroy the water hose or your plumbing. This should keep your water pressure down to a safe level.

Heavy Duty Extension Cord

There is never an electrical outlet nearby.

Refrigerator Door Lock

There is nothing more trouble than the refrigerator door opening during a trip.

Campground Directory

A good one will give all public and private campgrounds as well as prices. They should also give directions and locations of free campgrounds.

Fire Extinguisher

Buy one of these or keep a supply of water around because some RVs are made of plastic and burn quickly.

Tips on Buying an RV

1. The RV market is small, seasonal, and therefore quite volatile. If you take your time and don't jump at the first opportunity, you should find an excellent deal.

2. In most parts of the country, RV sales and prices are tied to the seasons. Demand, brought on by the impending vacation season, picks up in spring and then falls off after August. In areas where hunting is popular, small RVs stay in demand until the end of hunting season. Very large motor homes are less seasonal and vary in price according to the introduction of new models.

   In the Southwest and Florida, where many spend the winter in RVs, prices are higher in the peak winter months. However, the larger supply of RVs means the market is more organized and there is less opportunity for a good bargain.

3. When you're developing a list of milestones, you should schedule your planned purchase for a season where the local market is depressed. Then be sure to give yourself at least three months to find something you like. Finally, don't be determined to buy during that time period. If you don't find something you like, just keep looking.

4. Before you start seriously looking, you should spend time looking at RV dealerships. That way you should have a good idea of what you want and the prices you will have to pay. Remember to stick to that price range and don't go higher unless you find something really special.

5. Private purchases are better than dealers. Some dealers promise a warranty period with a purchase, but that's rarely worth anything (especially if you're travelling outside the region). These repairs are usually slipshod and only good enough to keep the vehicle running past the warranty period.

6. When you're looking, cover all the possible markets. Look at the classifieds, RV magazines, local auto and truck trading periodicals, even driveways where an RV may have a "for sale" sign.

7. When you're seriously looking, have the money readily available. Nothing can drop a price faster than telling the sellers that if you receive your price, you can have a certified check in their hands before the end of the day.

8. Check the vehicle out thoroughly. Don't take anything for granted. Don't let the seller bamboozle you with, "Oh, that's easy to work. You just turn it on." That's a warning that it may not work. If they say it can't work because there isn't propane, take it out and buy a couple of dollars of propane (providing you're serious about the vehicle). *Check everything!* Turn the refrigerator on and check it out a couple of hours later. Be sure it can work on both propane and electricity. Before you finalize the purchase, review everything so you don't have any questions.

9. After you buy it, take it out on some weekend or day trips. Be sure you enjoy this lifestyle and decide what changes must be made to make you happy. You can spend the time between your purchase and the time you leave to remodel the RV and become comfortable with a mobile lifestyle.

10. Even if you're storing the RV elsewhere, use it as often as you can. Our RV was stored near where I worked, so my wife and I would use it as a meeting place for any activities after work. We would even spend Saturdays just watching TV and eating there in order to become comfortable in it.

Summary

Most of the people who couldn't adjust to a mobile lifestyle made their mistake when they bought the RV. If it's too small, you will soon yearn for your old house. If it's too large, you will not be able to live in the wilderness. Most important, if you've ignored the comforts, you will surrender and return to the world of governments, community standards and the rat race.

5

Living Cheap

"Those who want the fewest things are nearest to the gods."
— **Socrates**

If by now you are wondering how anyone can live so inexpensively that a low paying job or occasional odd jobs are enough, this chapter is for you. It will show you ways a person can live for less than any social worker would admit is possible and prove that the American welfare system is a fraud forced on the taxpayers.

Eating For Less

"A hungry man is not a free man."

— Adlai Stevenson

Most of the hunger in America is based on ignorance, not a lack of money. Hunger relief advocates insist that the 1990 food-stamp allotment of $75 per week for a family of four is too little and should be increased to over $100. Yet my wife and I live on $30 a week and enjoy many luxuries. We can even cut that by 50% and still eat nutritious, enjoyable meals. And, if necessary, we could cut that down to as little a $7 a week if we wanted to give up some expensive foods like cheese.

So why are so many people supposedly starving in America? The first problem is that they are victims of merchandising; they would rather buy what's advertised on TV than what's good for them. The second problem is the social welfare bureaucracy that needs to insure a future supply of hungry Americans so they can keep using tax-payer money to live their expensive lifestyles in Washington, DC. If they taught the hungry how to feed themselves, many programs would disappear because all Americans could eat with little or no money.

Americans have forgotten what their pioneer forefathers did. One hundred years ago most families went to the store for just a few basics. Then they combined these basics with the produce of the land to prepare food that was both nutritious and cheap. If we did the same thing, our food bills would shrink and we would avoid the fatty, high cholesterol foods that cut years off our lives.

The Freedom Road lifestyle fits perfectly with cheaper and better eating. Since money isn't your god, you have the time to fix enjoyable meals in your RV and hunt for tasty foods in the wilderness. You can end up with meals that are the envy of your "richer" friends. You might even make some money selling unique foods to those people too lazy to make them themselves.

What this section discusses is the essentials of inexpensive eating. In *Appendix I*, I have included recipes that our ancestors and modern day pioneers use to eat well for less. Many of these recipes cost less than a dollar a day.

Basic Foods

There are a couple of dozen foods that should be found in your kitchen. Since many are commodities, you can shop around and even buy them for considerably less at a food wholesaler. However, you will still save money even if you buy them at the supermarket.

Pinto Beans. Mexicans and the Indians of the Southwest know that anyone with a bag of pinto beans in the house will not go hungry. They are extremely versatile and I have seen everything from fudge to a meat loaf substitute cooked with them (see *Appendix I*). If you combine beans with a corn dish, you have a meal that supplies virtually all the needed amino acids. Although prices vary according to the amount you buy, this food is an excellent place to start if you want to spend less than a dollar a day.

Rice. This is a basic food for most of the world and it's easy to see why: it's inexpensive and can be eaten in an infinite number of ways. Although Americans prefer white rice, brown rice still has the hull and more vitamins (brown rice doesn't become sticky like white rice, either). Rice and pretty nearly any leftover or vegetable will make a tempting casserole. If you combine rice and beans, you have a basic meal that has all the necessary proteins. To save money, find the local Chinese grocery and buy this grain in bulk.

Powdered Milk. You can use this for drinking, cooking, and even making yogurt. It has less calories and fat than regular milk. This is a must for any milk drinker who wants to live in the wild because it takes up less space. I use it to add a creamy texture to casseroles.

Powdered milk can have a strange taste if you don't prepare it properly. Use a large two quart jar, fill it halfway with water and add the powder. Shake vigorously and let the foam settle. Then fill the jar with cold water. Since this milk improves as it sits, you should let it age a day or so before drinking.

Potatoes. If you're Irish, you know this can keep you going for years. Potatoes are often found on sale for as little as 95¢ for 10 lbs. at supermarkets. Keep an eye out for these specials and you'll never go hungry. Potatoes will keep best if you store them in a cool, dark, well ventilated place.

Onions. They last a long time although we use them so much they don't get the chance in our motor home. The inexpensive yellow variety have a good flavor in addition to nutrition. I add them to about any meal I cook.

Carrots. Like onions, they last a long time. They are a great snack and can be cooked even after they're dried out. Every kid who listened to their mother knows about the vitamins they contain.

Olive Oil. Although the Greeks and Italians have high fat diets, they have less heart disease than Americans. Experts know olive oil is responsible for this. Although I use very little oil in cooking, this is one of the healthiest.

Pasta. This is frequently found on sale in most grocery stores. Buy them when they are on sale and don't worry about the shapes. They are a good base for casseroles and soups.

Flour. There are all sorts of flour, but stay away from the conventional white flour. I use corn, whole wheat and oats to make biscuits and cookies.

Oats. It's a good breakfast cereal in addition to an ingredient for some of my favorite breads. It used to be dirt cheap until it became a health food fad. Since it's a popular feed for animals, you can buy whole grain from most feed stores for a fraction of what it would cost in a health food store.

Honey. Although expensive, it's one of the best sweeteners. It adds much more flavor than regular sugar. Don't worry if it crystallizes. Just warm the jar up in hot water.

Cheese. It's high in fats and cholesterol, but it's a good source for calcium and protein. If you store it properly, it will last a long time. We find a little bit adds a lot to most meals, especially casseroles. Since I hate milk, this is my substitute.

Ground Turkey. Although it costs about the same as hamburger, turkey has more protein and less fat. Since it has little fat, I can add it to casseroles without worrying about cooking and draining the fat first.

Mung Beans. Many Chinese dishes use bean sprouts and you can sprout your own for a fraction of their cost in the store. They contain many vitamins and they can keep your food bill under a dollar a day. They can be found at health food stores.

Alfalfa Seeds. I was in Alaska, seventy-five miles from the nearest green plant. We made a delicious salad with alfalfa sprouts, oil, vinegar, and parmesan cheese. These seeds sprout anywhere and contain all the vitamins you need.

Spices. Spice is the soul of food. You can take basic foods and make a nearly infinite number of dishes with the creative use of spices.

Garlic. This is one of the best spices you can use. Many doctors now say it's good for your heart and the immune system.

Soy Sauce. There are few dishes cheaper and tastier than vegetables, rice and soy sauce.

Chili. Chili powder and beans are the basis of many Mexican dishes.

Bullion. Beef and chicken bullion are good starters for many inexpensive soups.

Buy in Bulk

With $100 I can buy 80% of the nutritional and calorie requirements for two people for a year. It's easier than you think, but most Americans only think about buying food at the supermarket. As with most things in this book, you have to change your thought patterns. Instead of going to the grocery store, visit a bulk food center or farmers' cooperative. There you can buy 50 or 100 lb. bags of rice, beans, nuts, honey, and grain. You can either store the food yourself, or you can split the larger purchases with a few other families. To start your search, look under health foods in the Yellow Pages. In order to store bulk food, I use plastic garbage bags and store them in a closed space so they can't be attacked by pests.

If you make an annual trip to a bulk food center, your trips to the grocery store should be limited to fresh vegetables, meats, and spices. With a little effort you can keep your total food bill under a dollar a day, if not lower!

Look to Nature

Buy a book on edible plants and start taking it with you as you walk. Although many of the plants are edible, not palatable, you should find a few real treats in the wilderness. For instance, why buy sunflower seeds when they often grow wild near abandoned bird feeders. You can collect them as they mature and sun dry them yourself. You can even use wild grains and seeds to add to your flour for baking. They add flavor and more fiber than the processed flour of the stores.

Learn to Make Casseroles and Soups

A casserole is nothing more than a filler such as rice, beans or pasta and something else. With it, you can stretch a couple of ounces of meat or vegetables to feed a family. The only art to making one is learning what goes with what.

As a rule, rice should be used with delicately flavored foods (like many vegetables), beans go well with beef and bacon, and pasta should accompany something that has a sauce (for example, cheese, milk, or tomato sauce). Soy sauce is an excellent flavoring for rice dishes while chili and garlic are good for bean dishes. Needless to say, garlic is a good flavoring for pasta.

Soups are also like casseroles because they can stretch food or be used to get rid of leftovers. Start with bullion for stock and then add any meat, bones, or vegetables you have left. As the soup simmers, add any seasoning you need. Soup is great for using dried vegetables or meat bones. If you need to thicken it, add rice, beans, pasta, or grains like barley.

Use Everything

Americans always waste food. They buy food and throw away anything that's tough, wilted, or looks unappealing. We try to use everything. Dried, wilted, or tough vegetables are saved for cooking in a casserole. Bones can be saved for a soup. Fat is given to the dogs (it's good for their coats and cuts down on dog food).

It also pays to look in the refrigerator occasionally to see if anything is going bad. If it is, use it before it has to be thrown away.

Learn to Cook Your Favorite Meals

We used to go to a restaurant every week for the same meal. When we decided to move into the RV, I knew I couldn't afford to keep patronizing the restaurant, so I learned how to cook the meal. Now we still eat the same meal once a week, but it costs a tenth as much.

Learn Cheap Luxury

Treat yourself to a really good meal once a week. For us it's salmon, fresh vegetables, and champagne. We take the time to prepare it and spend time enjoying it. Just use one of your cookbooks as a menu and decide what to order. Then next time you go to the store, buy the ingredients. Then on a special day take the time to prepare it and serve it properly. You would be surprised how much you enjoy this special event.

Inexpensive Drinks

Soft drinks are too expensive and water is too bland, so why not find something else? Tea is a good choice because it's good both hot and cold (if you are staying in a very hot area like the desert, don't drink tea because it dehydrates you). If you collect food from the wild, you can make some of your own teas with wild mint. A good way to liven up water is to add a small slice of lemon to it. It freshens the water and adds some vitamin C.

Alcoholic drinks are very expensive and can damage the body. If you want to drink, the best choice is wine. You can buy some inexpensive domestic table wines for a fraction of hard drinks. There are many scientists who say a moderate amount of wine is good for your health.

Vitamins

I believe vitamins are best consumed in your food. However, an inexpensive bottle of generic multivitamins can help balance a poorly balanced diet.

Eat Local Dishes

Mexican food is cheap in the Southwest. There is usually a whole section for tortillas at the grocery store and they are so cheap that you may want to use them instead of bread. However, if you try the same thing in Boston, the selection will be worse and the tortillas will cost more. Of course, the seafood can be fresher and cheaper in Boston (if anything is cheap in Boston).

When you travel to a new area, check the grocery stores for local delicacies. If you see something new, ask someone at the store how to cook it — chances are they will be able to tell you.

Cutting Travel Costs

Don't plan on spending all your time travelling across the country unless you're rich because RVs are gas hogs. Even if you travel with a trailer and unhook it, the large engine of the vehicle will still require a lot of energy to move. Therefore, you need to cut your costs considerably, especially if you're living on a limited budget.

Drive Directly to Your Objective

Don't become involved in side trips unless you weigh the cost. For instance, a 100 mile detour may be more scenic, but if your rig gets 10 mpg, the cost of the trip is more than $10. That may be a high price to see some nice scenery and you could probably enjoy the money in a better way.

Shop for Gasoline

Freeways and remote gas stations are poor buys for gasoline. If you're staying in a city, where gas prices are competitive, fill up before you leave. If you're driving on the freeway and you need gas, have the copilot use binoculars to check the advertised prices as you near the turn off. That gives you more time to decide whether to stop. Remember that as little as a 2¢ price per gallon difference will mean a dollar in the price of a fill-up.

Fix Meals While Travelling

One of the advantages of driving a motor home is that the other person can prepare a meal while moving. This allows you to travel farther in a day and cut costs by limiting grocery bills and unnecessary driving to restaurants.

Drive at a Reasonable Speed

As much as I hate the 55 mph speed limit, I usually stick to it when I drive the motor home. As you travel faster than 55, the wind resistance increases dramatically and you need more gasoline.

Plan Trips

When you go out shopping in your RV, plan your itinerary so you use less gasoline. Sometimes we park in a central place and walk to the stores we want to visit.

Pick Your Location

If you want to travel to avoid winter, you can save money by living in the West where half a day's travel can take you from an ideal winter home to an ideal summer home. For instance, you can live near Phoenix, Arizona in the winter and enjoy mild temperatures. Then in the summer, you can travel half a day to Flagstaff where the summers are comfortable.

Cutting Your Camping Costs

You may think camping out in the wilds is free, but you're mistaken. While there are millions of acres of government land where you can camp without a fee, it's far from free and you will incur some costs, especially if you decide to stay longer than a week or two.

The most common problem for the freedom seeker who wants to stay in one place is the park ranger. The government frowns on people who live in RVs, not in houses. In order to restrict their number, they usually have limits on the time you can stay in one place. That means eventually, unless you find a remote spot, someone is going to come to your door and ask you to move on. If you keep darting around an area, the rangers will inevitably recognize your vehicle and start to cause trouble. Then you will have to move out and spend more on gasoline.

Fortunately, not all government land is popular national parks or forests. There are many areas in the national forests or other government lands, where officials are less likely to find you. If you keep your rig in good shape and it's tourist season, you can probably convince any official that you're just on vacation. Just be sure you haven't changed the surrounding area in such a way as to make them disbelieve you. We will look at places to stay with a minimum of hassle in Chapter 10.

If you're planning to stay out in the wilderness, there are some costs that still can't be avoided. If they prove to be too high, you may want to move elsewhere or even think about staying in an RV park for awhile.

Power

Depending on your need for luxuries, electricity may become a major limitation on staying out in the wilds. If you only use the lights sparingly, you can live on your battery system and your generator indefinitely. However, if you enjoy the TV or your job requires power (as a writer, I need electricity for my word processor), you will find yourself using your generator more than you should. You can buy an invertor that converts 12 volt DC to 120 volt AC. That will allow you to use some AC appliances, but you will have to recharge the battery more often.

Another choice if you use a great deal of electricity is to stay in an RV park on occasion. Then you can do those things that need power all at one time.

The best alternative for your power needs is the most expensive. You can buy some solar cells to recharge your batteries. Depending on the size of the array you buy and the solar energy available, you can even operate small 120 volt appliances with such a system and an invertor. These systems are very expensive if you buy them "off the shelf," however, if you buy the solar cells in bulk and wire them yourself, you can make the cost of solar power competitive. For instance, if you buy your solar cells from a manufacturer, you should be able to make a solar cell arrangement for as little as $6.25 a watt (that assumes 1991 prices and units of at least 100 watts).

Communications

If nothing else, your profession may require you to stay in contact with others. Writers and photographers must talk to customers and people who live on the flea market circuit must make reservations and contact vendors. Unfortunately, when you camp out, you're totally out of touch unless you have a beeper or a mobile phone. Even if you have one of those, they may not work in a very remote spot.

If your heart is set on living deep in the wilderness, you should be sure any job you have will allow you to stay out of contact for awhile.

Water and Dumping

Depending on your habits and where you live, acquiring water and dumping sewage could be major problems. You could use a filter and take the water from a stream while making a system that processes your sewage (see the books listed in *Appendix II*). This will make you relatively independent from civilization. However, if you stay in a desert or you can't handle human waste and dirty water, you may have to go somewhere every few weeks to pick up water and dump waste.

Insurance

One of the biggest cons in the United States is insurance. We grow up with the idea that all responsible people insure themselves against everything. If you don't have insurance, others immediately assume you're an irresponsible person. As a result, Americans are the most overinsured people in the world. But in the final analysis, we aren't any better off and may actually suffer because of it.

Insurance breeds contempt for the danger. Would a smoker be as likely to continue his habit if he knew the chances of medical care would make him poor? Would a teenage driver be as reckless if any damages came out of his money? Would you think more carefully about fire hazards if your house and possessions didn't have coverage? If we had to face the dangers of this life, we would probably be more likely to avoid them.

The answer to insurance is self-insurance, where you foot the cost and save the premiums. Instead of buying homeowners insurance for your motorhome and possessions, look at the alternatives. Instead of spending hundreds in premiums, invest in a few fire extinguishers, fire alarms and burglar alarms. Then check your place to find any hazards and discuss how you would fight a fire. That will lessen the odds of a catastrophic occurrence.

The other reason for insurance is to protect yourself from liability suits if you're careless. However, the two ways to protect yourself from suits are: don't be careless and don't buy insurance. Today, suits are filed for profit, not justice. No one in their right mind will sue you because they tripped over a rock in your yard if you don't have insurance. There isn't any profit in it. Besides, a jury is less likely to find for the plaintiff if there isn't an insurance company footing the bill.

When deciding what insurance you need, keep in mind the alternatives. If you're healthy and live a healthy life-style, you can think about cutting out health insurance. If you scarcely drive and are a careful driver, it might make sense to register your car in a state that doesn't require insurance. And, if you are careful about fires and thefts, you can avoid fire and theft insurance. If you take these precautions, your life will be better and your insurance bill less.

One final thought on self insurance. Emergencies always happen and it makes sense to be prepared. Consequently, you should have a nest egg in case of an emergency. If you need to save some money for this insurance fund, just set aside the money you used to spend on premiums.

Storage

Depending on how much junk you accumulated over the years, you will probably have too much to put into an

RV. Even after donating to charity and giving to relatives, there will still be a collection of stuff you want to keep. The best suggestion is to rent some storage space. Depending on the location and the amount of space, these storage places cost $25 a month and up. But, no matter how small the cost, there is a good chance you will tire of spending the money and in a couple of years will sell or give away the rest of the junk.

Entertainment

Many of the libertarians who tried to live in the wilderness and failed didn't realize that entertainment is an important part of our lives. Either they spent too much time working or they tired of the spare time they had. A little preparation will give you many inexpensive hobbies and diversions to make life more enjoyable.

Television

People make fun of the overwhelming influence of the "boob tube" in our lives, but they fail to realize its importance. It's an excellent source of news and entertainment, especially if you can ignore the advertisements. Unfortunately, it has a couple of disadvantages for the Freedom Road lifestyle. The first is electricity. If you don't want to turn the generator on every time you use the set, you can buy an inexpensive TV that uses 12 volt DC. The picture is usually small and it may be inconvenient for several people to watch for a couple of hours, but it's excellent for watching the news or something brief.

The biggest problem I've had with the TV is poor reception in remote areas. There isn't much you can do about this unless you bring along a satellite dish or a large antenna. If you intend to stay in one area for a long time, you might want to think about buying a better antenna.

Video Recorder

Even in the most remote areas, the TV can still be useful if you have a video recorder and some recorded tapes. In our case, we brought over two hundred films along with us and it's likely we will be watching a video tape when the TV is on.

As you plan your Freedom Road lifestyle, you might want to spend some time finding favorite films when they are on TV and taping them for future use. Then, when you leave, you will have something for those nights when you want to watch TV, but there isn't anything to watch.

Radio

Radios draw less power than a TV, offer more variety, and reach more remote areas. If you can afford it, you might want to buy a shortwave radio. In addition to conventional broadcasts, you can receive international radio like the BBC. Since shortwave broadcasts are bounced off the atmosphere, they will reach into remote valleys that can't receive conventional radio. Once, near Gunnison, Colorado, we could only receive the BBC (British Broadcasting Corporation) because it was the only signal that could find its way into the narrow, remote canyon we were staying in.

Books

There is no better entertainment than reading a book. Unfortunately, they can be a problem. First of all, they are expensive (why should I complain, I get a royalty). I'm a fast reader, so I can consume a $4 paperback in a day. That's more than I can afford on my Freedom Road salary.

The library is a solution to the cost of books, but if you travel too much you can't qualify for a library card. Fortunately, there is a solution for the traveler. First check thrift stores for used books. You can often find popular books for a fraction of their original cost. Another good source for books is the RV park. Often you will find a pile of books in the laundromat that you can exchange for ones you have already read. Of course, you won't find many "quality" books in these places (by quality, I mean *my* books), but the price is right.

Exchanging books also solves the other problem with books: the space they take up. Unless you have some way to get rid of the ones you've read, your RV may start to look like the bookmobile of the local library. If you built up an impressive collection, you might find a used book store willing to exchange them for some of their books. Or you might find another soul on the road with the same problem and you can exchange your hoards.

One final recommendation on books. Buy a couple of used textbooks on subjects you'd like to know more about. A good textbook can't be read quickly and should teach you the subject even though you aren't taking the class. With a little patience you can have the equivalent of a college course for the cost of an old textbook.

Conversation

The TV and the radio have ruined the fine art of conversation. However, you can bring this inexpensive entertainment back by applying just a few rules.

Be less interested in yourself and more interested in others. Many people have had interesting lives that they would share if someone listened and showed interest.

Frame your questions to elicit a discussion, not just an answer. Instead of saying, "nice day today," why not rephrase the question to something that will inspire conversation. If you ask, "Why is the weather always beautiful around here," chances are you will start a conversation.

Learn to be curious about other skills. We often concentrate on the skills necessary to do our job, but have you ever thought what it takes to do another job? Maybe you can learn something useful. Ask someone about their job, why it's rewarding and what the challenges are.

Hobbies

The Freedom Road lifestyle is a great opportunity to develop a hobby. Maybe for the first time in your life you will have the opportunity and time to pursue a special interest. As I will show you in the next chapter, a hobby can make money in addition to being fun.

Summary

"Far better it is to dare mighty things, to win glorious triumphs, even though checkered by failure, than to take rank with those poor spirits who neither enjoy much nor suffer much, because they live in the grey twilight that knows not victory nor defeat."

— **Theodore Roosevelt**

The old saying, "A penny saved is a penny earned," is very true in the Freedom Road lifestyle. Since one of the things we are trying to escape is the tyranny of a dull job, it scarcely makes sense to spend so much that you're forced to take a job you don't like. By carefully applying this chapter, your financial needs will be less, you will have more opportunities to make enough money, and you will have the time to enjoy life to its fullest.

6

Earning Money

"Nothing is really work unless you would rather be doing something else."

— **James Matthew Barrie**

No matter how well you apply the previous chapter, you'll need some money. But there isn't any reason that you can't have fun while earning it, especially if your needs are simple enough.

Earning money in the Freedom Road lifestyle isn't work, it's fun. You can do something you like, maybe just work part-time. If you work in your RV, you avoid the hassles of commuting. Finally, you make more efficient use of your time because you can move from work to leisure as necessary. You will never be stuck at a desk twiddling your thumbs again.

Of course, working while you travel does have some problems and we should mention them now. The first is that you can't travel and work at the same time. If you intend to be a full-time nomad, picking up every morning and driving, you will not have the time to work. Consequently, you must balance your desire to travel with your need to stay put and make money. In my case, I usually limit my travel to one day a week. That gives me up to six days to work.

Another problem with earning money on the road is that you don't stay in one place long enough to build a reputation, advertise, or build a customer base. That forces you to either stick to a business where you have an established group of customers, or a business where finding new customers isn't a problem (swap meets and such).

The Basics

Unfortunately, business schools don't address the problem of a mobile business, so you have to learn as you go. Here are a few rules for the traveling businessman:

Stay In Contact With Your Customers

Don't drop out of sight or you will lose their business. Use the phone and mail to stay in regular contact. If possible, give them a number where they can reach someone who can contact you within a few days. Value clients with toll-free numbers; they allow you to stay in contact without spending your money.

Anticipate Your Customers' Needs

Since you aren't just a phone call away, the customer can't call when they need something, so you should anticipate their needs and call before they arise.

Make Contacts as You Travel

One advantage of travel is that you meet more potential customers. Use your travel to contact small businessmen and others that may need your services.

Cater to High Quality Customers

Cheap, slow paying customers aren't worth keeping. Constantly review your customer base and remove slow payers, people who rarely buy, and people who offer little hope of future business. Then use the time you gained to acquire new customers and give old valued customers the attention they deserve.

Provide a Good Product

Since you can't pick up new customers easily, you need to keep your clients happy. The best way to keep customers happy is to give them high quality products, and a little more. The cost of keeping a customer is lower than the effort to acquire a new client.

The key to earning money on the road is to plan in advance. If you want to write or sell photographs, you must become a reliable source of material that customers will prefer. Earning that reputation usually takes years. Even selling at a flea market takes preparation because you must find a product, build an inventory, and learn how to work the shows.

This chapter can't tell everything you need to know about earning money. I will only outline some attractive professions for the traveler. If you want to learn more, there are several books (many sold by this publisher) that describe these jobs in detail. Just like everything in this book, there isn't any secret to success. You must plan in advance and have the determination to succeed.

Writing and Photography

Of all the road jobs, writing and photography are probably the most desirable. You work where you want and when you want. However, many feel such a dream occupation is beyond them. In fact, earning money in these fields is not hard if you're willing to apply yourself and don't expect to make it rich.

Although talent and knowledge are important to becoming a writer or photographer, skills can be acquired and they aren't the most important factor for success. The one overriding ability professional writers and photographers have is the discipline to finish the job on time without excuses. If you have that, you can succeed in this business even if you can't tell the difference between a split infinitive and a split screen.

Imagine you're a publisher and every month on the l5th you have to send your publication to the printer. If someone promises a piece for you and doesn't deliver before your deadline, you have to scramble and find someone who will fill the empty space. Invariably that other piece isn't as good and you probably had to pay a premium price to have it finished in a short time. It makes more sense to find someone reliable who will always meet deadlines. The unreliable writer/photographer may be better, but that quality doesn't mean anything if it doesn't arrive on time.

That's the key to successful writing: deliver good material on time and without excuses. If you're a good writer and can find interesting subjects to write on, you will have enough business to keep you traveling.

Building Your Career

If you need a few years to pay your debts, your chances of becoming a successful writer or photographer are better because it takes time to become established and cultivate customers.

The best analogy to entering the writing/photography field is baseball. You usually don't start with the Pittsburgh Pirates or in a major magazine like *Smithsonian* on your first try. You have to work your way up the ladder through the minor leagues before you have your first at bat in the major leagues.

The publishing business has an unofficial minor league system where major writers are first published. They start writing for minor publications with a few thousand subscribers. As the writer's style improves, they move to larger publications, using the better articles as proof of their skill. If they stay with it, in a few years they can be found writing for a major publication (I define the majors as any publication you can readily find at the local newstand).

Even if you don't make the publishing majors, don't give up. Just as there are thousands of baseball players that never made the majors, but made a living playing at a lower level, there are writers and photographers that make a satisfying living, without writing one major article.

As you work your way through the minors, take the time to develop contacts and keep working for publications that you like and that use your material regularly. Although they don't pay as well as the majors, you should have a "string" of publications you work for regularly. That will give you a monthly salary you can count on and keep your workload even.

On the Road

Once on the road, consider every new location a new opportunity. First investigate the area and find any points of interest that you can write or photograph for one of your regular publications. Then look for any opportunities that would let you produce something for a larger publication.

A new location means more customers. Check local publications and learn if they use any work by freelance writers or photographers. Even if they have a staff, there is still plenty of opportunity for special editions, where the larger size requires freelance work.

Talking For a Living

Every month thousands of societies, clubs, fraternal organizations, and professional groups have a meeting. If you were ever the meeting organizer, you know the challenge of finding entertaining shows. Usually, members are strong-armed into making talks and the result is a boring meeting that discourages members from attending future ones.

Now you can solve the meeting chairman's problem, improve meeting attendance, and make some money for yourself (even get a free meal thrown in) by becoming a professional speaker. You make $50 to $100 for an hour talk and you can use the same presentation again and again.

First find an interesting subject you have some experience with (say, living in an RV). Then write up a speech and illustrate it with loads of slides. Try the speech on a friendly crowd and revise it with their suggestions. When you're ready, call the presidents of some local groups or a local speakers' bureau and see if they're interested. If you present yourself properly, they will be glad to give you the business.

Once you start travelling, you will have to coordinate your speaking engagements and travel schedule (many speakers' bureaus will do this for you). Remember when you travel with an RV, your fuel costs are higher and you must charge for any trips that take you off your course.

Keep Your Old Job

If you like your present job and your employer likes your work, you might be able to keep working part-time on the road. Although most employers hate to admit it, there are many white collar jobs like software writing, consulting, etc. that can be done anywhere. If your present employer would be in a pinch if you left, he might agree to hire you on a part-time basis while you're on the road. This option would allow you to start your Freedom Road lifestyle faster and earn more money than with other jobs.

Construction

Probably the most mobile skills are those in the construction industry. I've know many men with construction skills who live in an RV and travel from one site to another. Although many of them prefer to live in one place, the jobs pay so well that they continue the nomadic existence.

One problem for travelling construction workers is state tax officials who check the sites for out-of-state residents. These bureaucrats aren't looking for people who need welfare, but someone they can force to pay state income tax. As far as they're concerned, you only have a right to a job if you're a resident of their state.

Making Your Hobbies Pay

You can make money from your hobby. Unfortunately, if you knit or do woodworking, don't expect to sell your products around an RV park. Many retired people have these hobbies and RV camps that cater to the retired have dozens of people competing with their wares.

You can profit from your hobby if you provide a service that others prefer to avoid. In my case, I collect Roman coins. When they are excavated in Europe, they're corroded and unrecognizable. I like to buy the dirty coins in bulk, clean them, identify them, and then either sell them to a dealer or to collectors. While many dealers and collectors avoid this task, I find it more enjoyable than just collecting the identified coins.

If you think about your hobbies, you can probably find a niche you can fill. If you travel a lot, you can meet others with the same interests by subscribing to a national newsletter and attending meetings in the locality.

Odd Jobs

Most businesses have jobs that need to be done, but they don't have the manpower or time. Since the chore is usually temporary, they won't hire someone just for the time it takes to complete the job. These are excellent opportunities for the traveler to make money.

Keep your eyes open for small jobs around businesses (like repainting lines in a small parking lot). Ask the owner or manager if they want the job done and offer a fair price. Depending on the type of business, you might offer to do the work in exchange for some of their products. In that case, you can make a better deal and probably close the sale faster.

You can also do chores around homes, but the pay is worse and the opportunities fewer. While businesses are willing to spend money to make money, most home-owners are too cheap.

Swap Meets and Flea Markets

Swap meets and flea markets are big business. People love visiting them because of their carnival atmosphere and the low prices compared to established stores. The vendors like them because they have low overhead and are part-time efforts. That allows people with full-time jobs or people who only want to work a few days a week to make money.

Swap meets are ideal for the Freedom Road lifestyle because they only take a few days a week, don't require advertising, and you can set up nearly anywhere in the United States.

The most important part of becoming a swap meet vendor is selecting your merchandise. The best suggestion is to visit a local meet and see what sells. Then, depending on your tastes, try to find a type of product you will be comfortable with. Obviously, if you are travelling, you want something small and not likely to break. If you are interested in swap meets, check *Appendix II* for books.

Panning for Gold

During the depression, many unemployed workers headed for the hills to pan for gold. The gold was in the streams and they didn't have to worry about unemployment.

Gold mining still attracts people. The West has many streams that contain gold and you can work for yourself (Mother Nature doesn't even hand out W-2 forms).

Don't be misled. Finding and mining placer gold (the type of gold found in streams) isn't the road to easy wealth. Although it isn't hard to find a stream with gold, acquiring ownership and obeying environmental laws make it harder than just dipping a pan into a stream and pulling out the gold nuggets. It's becoming even more difficult because the government is limiting exploration and mining in many parts of the country.

Although hunting for gold isn't a way to become rich, if your expenses are low you can make enough money to get by. Many national lands that aren't open to mining still allow "recreational panning." If you look like a vacationer just having a good time, park officials probably won't bother you.

Work at an RV Park

Many RV parks count on retired people, living in RVs, to provide the extra help during the peak seasons. Usually in exchange for rent, they hire people to work at camp stores or offices. Sometimes there is enough work for forty hour work weeks, for a few months. The pay isn't very good, but you never have to worry about commuting.

Summary

"Resistance to tyrants is obedience to God."

— **Thomas Jefferson**

A Freedom Road lifestyle requires some work, but the hours are of your own choosing and the work can be fun. If you want to enjoy your new life, be sure to find an occupation you like. If you aren't careful, you'll find yourself having fun all the time.

7

Finding A Place To Stay

"No one can build his security upon the nobleness of another person."

— **Willa Cather**

If you're already imagining yourself on the open road, breathing the air of freedom, it might be time to deflate your balloon a little. Even on Freedom Road, the minions of the state are working to make your life miserable. If you truly want freedom, you will have to leave the road sometimes.

The philosophical argument for mandatory payments like taxes is that government services available to everyone should be paid for by everyone. Of course, if you believe that, you may receive an "A" in your civics class, but you will fail in life. There is no better example than the road system.

Although gasoline taxes and license fees pay for some roads, much of the money comes from the taxpayer, whether they use them or not. Yet, when it comes to using the road, the state has declared its use to be a privilege, not a right. They reserve the right to refuse a license to anyone even though they virtually force citizens to have a drivers license for identification.

The bureaucrats think they own the road and the Supreme Court is helping them by allowing unconstitutional methods of search and seizure on the roadways. While the courts have allowed some protection to the individual in the house, they have ruled that protection against search and seizure in a car is virtually nonexistent. The police can set up check points (like in Nazi Germany), they can stop you for no reason (they will just tell the judge they thought one of your lights was broken), and they have greater latitude to search your car. If you long for the iron discipline of Hitler and Stalin, just visit America's roads. There is no better example than the recent Supreme Court ruling that even though drunk driving roadblocks only find 1 in 100 driving under the influence, the war against drunk driving is so important that it warrants a restriction of Constitutional liberties. The Gestapo (who could probably boast a similar dismal record of arrests at their roadblocks) used the same excuse for their actions during WW II.

The Law

These are just a few of the hassles you will face while on the road.

Licenses

The police want everybody and everything to carry up-to-date papers. Not only does it give the state more money, it provides an excellent excuse for stopping vehicles and harassing the owners. Not only must all the registrations be up-to-date, they should be from the same state. If your drivers license is from one state and the car title is from another state, you will be forced to explain.

There are no easy solutions to this problem. However, you should remember there isn't a law against someone from one state owning a car from another state as long as it isn't used regularly in the driver's state. State governments don't like it because they want the revenue themselves, but remember there isn't any law against owning property in another state. As long as you're "vacationing" in one of the other 48 states, you should have few problems.

Checkpoints

They tell us that the difference between the United States and the Soviet Union is that we don't have police checkpoints that restrict movement and check papers (they also tell us that taxes are voluntary). In this great country we can move anywhere and never show an ID.

In this great country I've been stopped by Immigration, state agricultural inspectors, and police checking on: safety inspections, up-to-date tax payments, valid registration, and drunk driving. There are also DEA agents who want to check out young people driving a motor home on a week day because they believe that anyone not working at a regular job must be selling drugs.

Police

Although RVs seem respectable, there are still risks for the driver in municipalities. This is where the police are seen as revenue enhancers. Here police wait for someone who breaks the slightest law ("I'm sorry sir, you didn't stay stopped long enough at that stop sign"). In order to placate the local population, most of the offenders are out of state and the arbitrary enforcement is justified as lowering the local tax burden.

In the past, men used to stop travelers and demand money for safe passage. They were called highwaymen and they could be shot on sight. Today their spiritual descendants are still extracting money from travellers, but they are called the police. They haven't changed much; refuse to deal with them and they will kill you.

Spending the Night

Although the "snowbird" phenomenon has changed some police attitudes, there are still some who don't like to see RVs parked. Spend an hour at the local mall and you risk a visit by a cop who will ask when you're leaving. In their mind, decent people live in houses and only "seedy" types would think of any other existence. Consequently, they see a parked RV as an attempt by some disreputable scum to settle down and ruin the community.

There are, however, some places you can spend a night while travelling and not spend money. If your RV looks respectable and you limit yourself to spending just the evening hours, you shouldn't be hassled.

Roadside Parks

Each state has rules governing how long you can stay in a roadside park. Some limit you to as little as an hour and some allow you to stay overnight. If you don't have a travel book that tells you, just check the rules posted at the park.

Although the police can be very strict when enforcing rules, there are some exceptions. If you're driving on a long stretch without stops, late at night, the police will probably let you stay long enough to grab a quick nap if for no other reason than safety. Weather conditions like snow, rain or high winds will usually make a highway patrolman relent because large vehicles are harder to handle in rough conditions.

Parks

Some state, local, and national parks have free overnight camping. However, the facilities are poor, they may be crowded, and they can be hard to find or out of the way. By the time you find one of these free spots, you may have wasted enough gasoline to afford staying at an RV park.

24-Hour Grocery Stores

These are my personal favorite. When we pull into a new town, we usually check the yellow pages to see where the stores are. We then find one in a good section of town and park after sunset. After settling in, we go shopping for groceries. Although I've never been hassled, I can show them I'm a customer.

In cases where we have been in a town for a few days, we have stayed at several stores (you will attract more attention and bad will if you spend two nights in a row at the same store).

Truck Stops

In order to attract business, many truck stops have a large parking lot in back that will accommodate truck drivers who want to fuel up and catch a quick snooze.

Although you don't have to worry about the hassles, a truck stop is scarcely the ideal place to spend a restful night. Noisy semis are usually pulling in and out all night long, the air is thick with diesel fumes, and the lots are well lit.

Take some time to look around a truck stop before you stop. Usually, you can find a spot removed from the traffic and smell. It can make the difference between a good night and one that made you wish you kept driving.

Stay Where You Do Business

It's the end of the day, you have just finished some business, and the owner is getting ready to leave. If he has the space, why not ask him if you can stay? Depending on his location, he'll agree and you have a free night.

If you're buying something, ask them to throw a few free nights in with the deal. It won't cost them anything and they might agree.

I also use this method when I travel on a writing assignment. While visiting a business for an article, I see if they will let me stay in the parking lot for free. They haven't turned me down yet.

Casinos

In order to attract customers, many small Nevada casinos offer free overnight camping for RVs. Of course, I like to give them some business, so I usually visit their inexpensive buffet during the evening.

Gas Stations

If it's late and you just filled up your tanks, ask the station owner or manager if you can pull out of the way and park for the night. After taking your $80, most will give you the okay providing you don't interfere with operations.

Staying For The Long Term

Thousands of people have declared their independence and found ideal places to live. Some of them have found communities where laws are less stringent and others have opted for total independence in the wilderness known only to a few friends. Where you choose depends on your needs and desires.

Any "permanent" location must be able to meet three criteria. The first and most important is legitimacy. It must appear that you belong or inevitably the cops will remove you. You can either acquire legitimacy by renting property, having the permission of the owner or appearing legitimate (a weekend vacationer).

The second factor is accessibility to the outside. If you need to shop each week, you better think about staying near a town instead of a hidden valley in the Rocky Mountains. Any long term parking must allow you to live a comfortable life without much effort.

The final criterion is the level of government authority evident or how often the area is patrolled. If you intend to stay on government land without permission, you should find a place where patrols are rare enough to limit risk.

Whenever you intend to settle down, consider your location in the light of these three factors. Obviously, there are trade-offs, but your location should maximize each of these three considerations. A wise choice will provide you with a location that you can enjoy for a long time.

Government Land

If you ever looked at a map of the Western United States, you know the largest land owner is the government. In fact, in some states they own a greater percentage of the land than the Soviets own in the USSR. Fortunately, for the freedom seeker, most of this land is rarely patrolled and you can often find a semi-permanent location. But, be warned. The bureaucrats frown on people living in the wilderness without permission. There are numerous stories of Interior Department officials driving people from public land. If you intend to stay on federal land, you should be prepared to keep quiet and appear to be a vacationer.

National Parks. These are the tourist traps of the government. Prices are high (especially if it's a popular park), the rules are onerous, and all you can see is the RV parked next to you. In addition, the park rangers are usually on the lookout for people who are trying to settle down. If you want to stay here to visit, go ahead. Just leave after seeing what you want.

National Forests. There are national forests that have RV facilities and all the amenities of a national park. However, much of this land is remote and rarely seen by government rangers. If you scout around, you can find a deserted road into a remote area where you won't be bothered for awhile.

Many of the people who live next to national forests consider the adjoining land to be practically theirs. If "trouble makers" start to camp on the land, they will probably tell the authorities. Consequently, if you intend to stay on public land for awhile, you should be on good relations with your neighbors or you should be out of sight.

Bureau of Land Management Land. There is quite a bit of land out west that doesn't belong to the forest or park system. It's rarely patrolled and you can even find a reason to stay on the land officially.

In many cases there are camping grounds that allow you to stay for a few weeks at a time. Some of these parks are popular with Freedom Road types or retired people. Although the facilities are crude (or nonexistent), the fees for staying are small or nonexistent.

One popular route for freedom seekers in the past has been to stake a mineral claim on 20 acres of land and then camp out. Unfortunately, the government has started to crack down on these people, even some legitimate mines. However, with an RV, you can probably convince any visiting official that you're only staying for a couple of weeks to prospect and do the required annual assessment work.

Hot springs and ghost towns are popular spots for Freedom Road types. Many have roads leading to them and some are popular with visitors. If you keep your rig looking like a vacationers outfit, you can stay in one of these places for a long time.

Las Vegas

Even the Freedom Road person who likes to meditate in the wilderness comes to the big city occasionally. In that case, I recommend Las Vegas because whatever you want is probably available and legal.

Las Vegas is probably the last of the "wide open" cities that populated the west. The local government understands limited regulation brings people to this town and they aren't in any hurry to add more laws. If you aren't too outrageous, there should be few problems with the law.

Gambling is the big attraction of Las Vegas, but the cost of living makes it a popular place for retired people. In order to attract gamblers to their casinos, most places offer discounts on food, lodging, and drinks. Many casinos offer low cost RV parks and buffets that only cost a few dollars. Providing you stay away from the gaming tables, you can enjoy fine RV accommodations, good food, and even entertainment for less than it costs to live a more modest lifestyle elsewhere.

Another reason to stay in Las Vegas is to establish residence. Since gambling taxes pay a large percentage of state expenses, there is no state income tax. That may not mean much money with a Freedom Road lifestyle, but it is one less tax hassle.

Snow Bird Areas

The snow bird phenomenon (retired people spending the winter in the south) creates many opportunities for the Freedom Road individual. Whole communities now count on fleets of RVs to bring them business each December. As a result, both the police and businesses treat RV owners with extra care.

Although the winter gives you the opportunity to blend in with the others, the summer offers many discounts. Some RV resorts are empty in the summer so they offer special discounts to attract guests. If you don't mind the heat, you can save some money and enjoy amenities like swimming pools, saunas, and whirlpools.

There are some places in the Southwest that have been overbuilt. As a result, you can often find RV parks that will offer discounts just to help cover costs.

Mexico

If you want to live the good life for a small amount of money, you might want to travel south of the border. The cost of living is dramatically lower and there are many places where the number of retired Americans makes it seem like the United States.

In order to spend some time in Mexico, you have to apply for a visa at the border crossing. Usually, all you need is proof of identity like a drivers license and you can automatically stay up to 180 days.

The one problem with Mexico is that they don't allow many items to be brought into the country. Firearms, cameras, and electronics, are items that are sometimes controlled. For instance, only one camera is allowed per person, so if you usually travel with two cameras and one video camera, you might be forced to leave one behind.

One way to enjoy Mexico and avoid the hassles of living there is to live near the border. This allows you to take advantage of the low prices across the border while enjoying the benefits of living in the United States.

Private Land Caretaker

Unoccupied land often becomes a junk yard for the locals. Unfortunately, the law doesn't punish the litterers, but the owners. You could contact someone who owns land and offer your services as a caretaker. You would promise to keep the place clean and be sure no one dumps on the land in return for a place to park. This solution offers you legitimacy without many restrictions.

RV Parks

RV parks are as different as their owners and there is probably one that fits you. Some offer many amenities while some are near the freeway, handle transients, and ask few questions. If you find one that meets your needs, ask the owners if they have a discount for staying for a few months or even a year. Most of them will quote a price that is often less than $100 a month.

RV parks offer mail delivery, pay telephones, message taking, and utilities; most of the conveniences of civilization without the cost. And, since you are living in your own RV, the managers aren't as concerned about your actions as an apartment manager might be.

If the travelling life is starting to wear you down, stop at an RV park for a few months. You can reestablish connections with the rest of the world, find a job, and even save some money. After a few months, you will probably realize why you started traveling in the first place and take off again.

Summary

Travelling every day may seem romantic at first, but inevitably the costs and the hassles will force you to spend more time at one place. The best idea is to keep travelling until you find a place you want to stay. One of our favorite "permanent" spots was where we stopped to spend Christmas and New Year. We were still there on the Fourth of July.

If you intend to stay on government land for awhile, remember the three criteria: legitimacy, needs, and authority. The government is bound to hassle anyone without a legitimate reason for staying on public land. You can either have a reason for staying (stake a claim), appear to be legitimate (a weekend camper), or avoid authority (stay in the boondocks). If you don't follow those rules, your "permanent" stay will be shorter than you think.

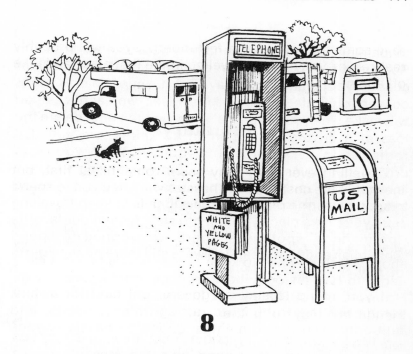

8

Links With The Outside

"They have rights that dare to maintain them."

— **James Russell Lowell**

A Freedom Road lifestyle may appear totally divorced from the outside, but there are many links that still bind you to friends, relatives, society, and government. Severing all of them may be harder than you realize. On the other hand, cutting a few select cords will give you much more freedom.

If you want to cut all links with the outside, try the Freedom Road lifestyle first and assure yourself that you are willing to make a complete break. This will allow you to maintain your contacts and re-enter society if Freedom Road isn't for you. If you break with the outside and later change your mind, you may find it impossible to live a conventional life again. For instance, two sacrifices you will make when you break all links with the outside are the loss of a drivers license when it expires and your RV registration. Of course, that doesn't keep you from driving, but the risks are greater. Since renewing a license is easier than applying for a new one, it makes more sense to keep this link instead of abolishing it.

Cutting your links also affects friendships and family relations more than most people realize. I don't know about you, but I need to keep all the friends I have. I can't afford to lose anybody because I lost contact with them. However, if you hate your family and don't have any friends, this may not bother you.

A major cost of the Freedom Road lifestyle is that you may never be hired for a good job again. Most employers expect their employees to have continuous employment histories and addresses. A two year gap in your life is usually considered a character flaw by most large businesses.

If, despite the problems, you still want to cut all bonds with the outside, you will want to look at some books offered by this publisher (Loompanics Unlimited). They can tell you how to disappear from your past and achieve more freedom. They can also help you establish a background if you later decide to return to society.

If, on the other hand, you want to maintain some contact, don't despair. You can acquire more privacy with little effort, yet keep those links you still want. After all, Freedom Road isn't a life of denial but a way to achieve more happiness.

State Residency

In totalitarian countries, people need up-to-date internal passports or identification papers. In addition, the government can insist that you remain the resident of a certain province even if you wish to move.

In the United States we have Social Security numbers and drivers licenses and it's legal for a police officer to ask to see them (even if you aren't breaking a law). In addition, some states, like California, are punishing people who have left the state for lower tax areas by continuing to tax them (these taxes have been declared legal by the courts). There isn't much difference, is there?

However, as of this writing, there isn't a law that forces you to declare residency in any state. Nor are the standards strict. For instance, President George Bush maintained a Texas residency by calling a hotel room in Houston his residence (he didn't even rent the room).

In fact, the only reason states want you as a resident is for the additional tax revenue you give them. If you can't pay any taxes or threaten to be a burden to their welfare system, they will use the law to deny your claim.

There is no better example of this attitude than California. Many people use tax breaks to save for retirement, but when they retire, they move to Nevada where there isn't a state income tax. The politicians needed a money fix so they sent bills for California income tax to the Nevada residents. They reasoned money earned in California must have income taxes paid even if the people moved before the taxes were due. Since they're forced to finance California's policies even if they disagree with them, the government is restricting a person's right to leave an oppressive government and enjoy a better life elsewhere.

But the hypocrisy of residency becomes obvious when you look at it another way. Suppose you worked in California and were fired. You're eligible for unemployment benefits (which were paid to the state by your employer). If you travel across the border to Nevada to live (because the cost of living is lower and jobs more plentiful), California would deny you any unemployment benefits because you're now a resident of Nevada. In other words, if you have money to give them, you are a resident, but if you need money, you aren't a resident.

Fortunately, this bureaucratic mindset is your salvation. If your earnings are low, you represent a money drain — not a source of revenue. If a government official says you're a state resident and you must register as such, thank them and ask them to certify it so you can go down to the welfare office and become eligible for benefits. They will probably change their mind and say that the welfare office should determine residency.

If no one is dictating your residency because you're poor, you can pick states that are more attractive because of tax laws or convenience. You can bank where there isn't a state income tax, title your vehicle in a state without property taxes on vehicles or a sales tax, and obtain your drivers license where it's most convenient.

Banking

Does someone living the Freedom Road lifestyle need a bank account? Probably not. As we mentioned in an earlier chapter, you shouldn't have much savings, no credit cards, and no outstanding loans. If you're dealing in small amounts of money and you have few out-of-town checks to cash, you can probably live without a bank. If you have a business where much of your income comes from checks, you will probably need to open an account when you move to a new spot or you should have one account with a regional bank that offers many branches and automated tellers.

If you don't have enough business to warrant a bank account, you can often manage with the following tips. An added benefit is avoiding many of the federal regulations and reports designed to find illegal money (illegal money is defined as any income that hasn't had taxes or a campaign contribution deducted from it).

Cashing Local Checks

A bank has to cash a check written on them, even if you don't have an account, as long as you have satisfactory identification. Consequently, if you receive some local checks, you can cash them with little problem.

Since the banks and the government are looking for large cash movements, you wouldn't want to cash large checks or make frequent visits to the same office. Otherwise you might attract some unwanted attention from the IRS or DEA.

Cash Checks at Local Stores

Many stores have a policy of cashing local business checks. Even if they don't, you may persuade the owner to cash checks you've received as long as you buy something from him.

Send Money Orders

Everybody needs to send money through the mail occasionally. Rather than have a checking account, buy money orders at supermarkets or convenience stores. In many cases, the cost of sending out a few money orders a month is less than the monthly charge on a checking account.

Travellers Checks

One safe, convenient way to keep money is to buy travellers checks. Like a personal checking account, they don't draw interest, but they are accepted most places. Although you may have to pay a charge for them, it is not much more than a checking account's monthly charge. In many cases, you may belong to an organization (like AAA) that allows you to buy them for free.

Mail

Receiving mail on Freedom Road is a blessing and a curse. The blessing is that since you don't have a permanent residence and probably aren't on many mailing lists, you avoid junk mail. The bad news is that friends and important mail will often have problems finding you. There are some solutions, however, that allow you to receive important mail and stay in contact with friends. They are:

Remail Service

This is the best (and most expensive) method for receiving your mail. You establish an address at a remailing service. They collect your mail and send it to you when you ask for it. You usually pay a monthly or yearly fee for the service plus an additional cost for postage.

These are popular with retired RV travellers and others who are on the move a lot. In many cases they also offer message services and can even help you establish a residence in a low tax state. Many of the services that cater to RV owners advertise in RV and travel magazines. Others can be found in the *Directory of US Mail Drops* published by Loompanics Unlimited.

Postal Boxes

If your travels are limited to one region and you find yourself travelling through one city constantly, you could rent a mail box either from the US Post Office or a private concern. Then, when you pass through, you can collect any mail that was delivered.

The problem with a mail box is that you will only receive your mail when you pick it up. On the other hand, if you rent from a private concern, you may be able to arrange forwarding if necessary.

General Delivery

If mail is infrequent and you can inform your correspondents about your location, you can have them send it to the local post office. If it's addressed General Delivery, the post master will keep it for two weeks and turn it over if you come in. This is perfect for people who have semi-fixed schedules and know they will be in a certain town at a certain time. Of course, in order for this to work, you have to keep people informed about your schedule.

This is also good for someone living in the wilds who comes into town every couple of weeks. They can receive mail without telling anybody where they live.

RV Park

If you're staying in a RV park for a few months just use the mailing address of the park. It doesn't cost anything and most parks have a box just for residents. Of course, since what you receive in the mail is known to the rest of the population, you might want to be careful about the type of magazines you receive. When you leave, just give a change of address to the post office (if you know where you're going).

Unofficial

If you receive a small amount of mail, you might be able to convince someone to hold it and remail it for you. It could be a friend, relative, or even a business that you deal with, if they're willing. If you follow this course, obey a couple of rules. First, keep the amount of mail and the work for your friend minimal. Second, don't have anything embarrassing sent to this address. Your friend may be upset when the Drug Enforcement Agency busts into the house because you ordered some drug paraphernalia through the mail.

Telephone

I've never missed the phone. Pay phones are abundant and I can have a good night's sleep in my RV without the interruption of a wrong number.

The best way to use the phone is to bring along change. You don't have a bill at the end of the month and you're aware of the cost as the operator keeps interrupting for more money.

If the person you're calling is interested in talking to you, they will probably tell you to call collect. You can even have them return your call by giving them the number of the pay phone.

If you're in the wilds and really need to stay in contact, you can buy a mobile phone, a beeper, or rent a remail service that takes messages. On the other hand, you may learn about the joys of writing letters.

Summary

The only real joys the rest of the world offers is friendship. Residency and banking are only fabrications of our society and have no value. Friendship, however, is important. That means that mail and phones are too important to eschew. Make plans to stay in touch with friends and family before you leave. As your lifestyle changes, your plans for staying in touch will evolve and inevitably you will learn how to avoid civilization without losing your friends.

9

Relationships On The Road

"I am the inferior of any man whose rights I trample under foot."

— **Robert G. Ingersoll**

Living With a Partner

Sharing the Freedom Road experience with a partner will either be a blessing or a curse. If you and your spouse are already having problems, a permanent life in a small RV could hasten divorce proceedings. On the other hand, if the two of you are really soul mates, Freedom Road could make your lives richer.

In our case, sharing a 28-foot motor home, 24 hours a day has been a wonderful experience. Without conventional jobs, we have more time with each other and the stress is less. We also eliminated any arguments about money (a major source of divorces) because we don't have any money to spend.

Of course, that doesn't mean eternal happiness is guaranteed if you move into an RV. In fact, some people who have travelled for a few months in an RV complain they were around their spouses too much. But, if you follow a few rules, a normally cramped lifestyle won't bother you.

Buy a Large Rv

Studies show everyone subconsciously creates a "neutral" zone around them. If someone invades this space, the subject becomes uncomfortable. The same thing happens in a small RV. The travellers are forced into each other's neutral zone and minor irritations will inevitably explode into full fights.

The best way to eliminate this problem is to buy a unit large enough for each person to find his or her own private corner. In our case, we have a motor home with two rooms. My wife can stay in the bedroom while I'm working in the living room. This way, we're still close to each other but we still have privacy and our own space.

Respect Each Other

While in the Navy, we had certain unwritten rules among friends. We respected each other's privacy and feelings. Sometimes this meant apologizing when I felt an apology wasn't necessary or ignoring certain subjects. But the result was fewer arguments in the cramped quarters of a ship. In the end, we had better working relations and spent many happy hours on liberty.

The same principle is true in an RV. Each person must try to defuse problems before they occur. If something is really bothering you, discuss it, bring it up in a friendly way, and try to work it out peacefully. If both people are willing, no problem is too large.

Share Responsibility

My wife and I were both in the Navy so we brought one Navy tradition to the RV: a captain. Each week at midnight Saturday, the other person becomes skipper for the week. As such, they are the final authority on spending, where we go, and what's served for dinner. Even though we scarcely ever disagree on what we should do, a rotating command gives each of us a chance to make all the important decisions. Not only does it eliminate arguments, it has provided many funny moments (Gee, I don't know what to do. I'm not paid to think this week.).

Make the Outdoors Part of Your Home

An awning, chairs, and other outdoor furnishings make the area outside your RV an extra living area. If the inside becomes too small for either of you, the outdoors can become another room.

Allow Each Other Privacy

Everybody needs to be alone sometime, so don't plan everything as a group activity. Allow the other person an opportunity to go somewhere alone. The free time will be good for both of you.

Making Friends on The Road

"If a man does not make new acquaintances as he advances through life, he will soon find himself left alone; one should keep his friendships in constant repair."

— **Samuel Johnson**

I can always tell a full time RVer from a weekender by the way they act. If I'm walking through a park and I see a new RV setting up I usually greet the owner. The weekenders will usually slink a look at me and maybe grunt a greeting before they return to their work. A full-time Road Bum, on the other hand, will usually stop and strike up a conversation. Usually before we finish talking, I know where they came from, the numbers and sex of their grandchildren (if any), and any other opinions they feel are important. By investing five minutes, I make a friend.

Modern life is so crowded and hurried that most people are too uncomfortable or too busy to make new friends. As a result, most Americans have a hard time meeting others, especially outside the work place. When thrust into a new environment they are unable to cope and often feel lonely. Its like someone starving in a corn field because they don't know how to cook.

Making friends on the road is easy if you just follow a few hints.

Greet Everyone

Everyone on the face of this earth is a potential friend. You'll never know which ones they are unless you start talking. I try to greet everyone I meet. If a new RV is setting up, I often wander over and try to start up a conversation.

One of the best openings is to look at the license and ask, "Where in ... are you from?" That will start the discussion. If you've been to the state, you can talk about your experiences or if you haven't, you can ask about the region. If the person you're talking to is a full time RVer, you'll have a new friend.

Sit Outside Your RV

Nothing stimulates friendship more than sitting outside and striking up a conversation with everyone that passes by. Before you know it someone will stop, sit down and talk with you. Just be sure to bring out enough chairs and something for everyone to drink.

Broaden Your Interests

I like writing, photography, baseball, rodeo, football, politics, science, in addition to many other subjects. Chances are that anyone I talk to will have some similar interest and we can have a fascinating conversation.

Be Willing to Learn

Even if we don't have a similar interest, maybe the other person can tell me about their interests or job. You will at least learn something new and maybe even acquire a new hobby.

Try to Make Friends with Everyone

Never say someone isn't going to be around long enough to be a friend. I've had good conversations with people who were preparing to leave. The only thing I regretted was that they were leaving just when I found out how nice they were.

Be a Good Conversationalist

The art of good conversation is to draw out the other person. That requires more than just asking questions that can be answered with a yes or no. Try to ask questions that require a detailed answer. For instance, if you see a sticker on the car that tells you the driver is a Pittsburgh Pirates fan, don't ask them if the Pirates are going to do well that year because that may elicit just a yes or no. Instead ask them how the bullpen will hold up. There isn't a baseball fan in the world that couldn't spend hours discussing the strengths and weaknesses of each of the five pitchers in the starting rotation. Even if you don't care that Clyde Haystomper has an ERA of 1.23 against left-handed hitting, you have certainly drawn the person into a conversation.

Each Person You Haven't Talked to is a Missed Opportunity

Unfortunately, I've missed many interesting people (or learned about them too late) because I didn't try to talk to them. There is nothing worse than finding someone who shares interests with you at the last minute (especially if they have been around for a few months).

Stay In Contact

Letters don't take long to write and a poorly written letter is better than no letter at all. Consequently, stay in contact with friends. You may have the opportunity to get together at a future date.

Summary

"The tragedy of life is not so much what men suffer, but rather what they miss."

— **Thomas Carlyle**

Freedom alone isn't enough. You must have relationships with others that make the freedom worthwhile. Fortunately, the Freedom Road lifestyle allows you more time to develop and nurture your relationships and remove much of the stress that often tears people apart. For the first time, you can enjoy and savor life and the people you meet. Soon you will wonder why you spent all that time working for money when you were wasting the time necessary to make friends.

10

Free People, Free Places

"You cannot depend on your eyes when your imagination is out of focus."

— **Mark Twain**

You aren't the first person to search for freedom. For centuries, others have left their homes and found new lands where they could express their own beliefs. Many of these refuges, like the United States, became reality and flourished while others, like New Harmony, Indiana floundered on the shoals of practicality. As a result, there is never a guarantee that any ideal place will exist for long.

This chapter can't identify the best place for you. Rather, I want to look at a few places in the United States where people have the opportunity to live outside the dictates of normal society. In each of these areas, people have a healthy disregard for government and a healthy respect for individuality. Chances are, if you visit each of these locations and look around, you will find a place where you can live the Freedom Road lifestyle.

Gunnison, Colorado

When my mind wanders, it often finishes near Gunnison, Colorado. Here it feasts on spectacular views reminiscent of the Swiss Alps, broad expanses of forested wilderness, and a breed of individual that harkens back to the era of the pioneers.

From Gunnison to Telluride, Colorado is relatively undeveloped. Outside ski resorts, the area is sprinkled with small towns that are little more than a gas station, post office, and a convenience store. Most people live in ranches in remote valleys and prefer that rugged life.

One of the advantages of this area is the reasonable summer temperatures. Gunnison is often the coldest place in the country and its summer temperatures are more like a comfortable spring day. As a result, you won't need an air conditioner during the summer.

One of the attractions for the Freedom Road lifestyle is the amount of government land in the region. National forests, parks, and wilderness make up about 90% of the land, so there are many areas an RV can stay without parking fender to fender with other RVs.

Although the people of the Gunnison area are individualists, they tend to be conservative, so hippie mobiles are definitely not the way to keep a low profile. Just keep a conservative facade, stay off their land (trespassing is a major sin in the West) and you should have few problems.

Although Gunnison is one of my favorite spots, there are a few problems for the Freedom Road person. The first is the cold weather. As I said earlier, it's often the coldest place in the 48 states; winter temperatures are extreme and snow is plentiful. As a result, the best time of the year is June through September. Any other time and you may be caught in snow or experience temperatures too cold for an RV.

Another problem with this region is the high altitude. Most RV equipment is designed for sea level. You may have to modify your carburetor, furnace, refrigerator, generator, and anything else that uses propane. Check your manuals for instructions.

Another disadvantage for larger RVs is the narrow roads that go into much of the government land. Although I've seen truck campers in remote locations, most larger RVs will have to stay closer to the road.

If these problems don't bother you, Gunnison and the surrounding area is one of the best places to live during the summer. Just be sure you leave before the snows come or you may be spending a cold winter.

Humboldt County, California

If Gunnison is too conservative for you and you long for the life of the 1960s, then Humboldt County and other parts of Northern California are for you. A visit to some towns in this area is about the closest thing to a step back in time, when people were "laid back" and psychedelic colors were in fashion.

Humboldt County, California, is also famous for marijuana. This is the marijuana growing capital of the US and the home of Humboldt Lightning, well known for its effect on the human nervous system.

Temperatures in Northern California are mild enough for year around living in a recreational vehicle and it has greater access to larger cities than many areas of the country.

The marijuana business is a mixed blessing. Most people in the area are individualists and willing to let others live their own ways. On the other hand, the government, in its war on drugs, has targeted the area and many nonconformists will become victims of the cops even if they aren't involved with drugs.

You can also get caught between the government and the growers if you aren't careful where you stay on government land. Booby traps can be found on trails and the government will assume you're guilty if you decide to camp near a pot crop.

However, the government insanity will finally end and this corner of California will return to normal. When it does, add this location to your itinerary.

Arizona Strip

There is still a place in the United States where polygamy is tolerated and taxes are considered evil. If a place like that appeals to you, try the Arizona Strip, the piece of Arizona north of the Grand Canyon and physically separated from the rest of the state by the Colorado River.

Although this land is part of Arizona, it's culturally and physically a part of Utah. If you want to visit the strip, you must travel through Utah and if you want to succeed, you should be a Mormon.

This is high country that can become cold during the winter and dry during the summer. Land is unproductive and you can't grow plants or raise much cattle unless you have access to water. But it's one place that is nearly forgotten by the government (either that or they don't care).

Most of the people who live here are Mormon, and they don't like outside authority. In fact, when the Mormon leadership disavowed polygamy in the late 19th century, those in southern Utah felt their leaders had veered from the true path. They feel the same about the US government. Here, many people feel taxes are wrong and don't even use US currency for transactions (often resorting to gold).

Be warned: this isn't an anarchistic region. The government in the area is run by the Mormons and the elders aren't tolerant. In fact, you may decide that the US government is easier to deal with. However, if you're conservative in appearance and actions, you may find this to be a nice place to stop.

Idaho

If you like the wilderness and people with a streak of individuality, your state should be Idaho. It has mountains, rushing rivers, clean air and people who enjoy such beauty.

Although it's known for its potatoes and fertile land, most of the state consists of tracts of wilderness that could swallow many Eastern States. In fact, it's not unheard of for policemen to have beats larger than New Jersey in this state. As a result, government interference is limited and you can go a long time without seeing the law.

The people of Idaho are worthy of their land. Here is a rugged individual who enjoys the outdoors and respects the rights of others. In most parts of the state, the unwritten law is to ignore your neighbor and don't ask questions.

The southern part of the state is the breadbasket and population center. Here you can buy fresh produce for a fraction of store prices or even buy a small inexpensive piece of land to try your own luck at gardening.

As you head farther north, the state becomes more remote and wild. If you're looking for a spot to park the rig for a few months and enjoy unspoiled scenery, this is the place. The chances are good that you will see few people during your stay.

Of course, an earthly paradise must have a flaw. In Idaho's case the winters can be bitter in many parts of the state. When the cold winds of November start to rage, you better start packing up.

Summary

"Write on my gravestone: 'Infidel, traitor.' — infidel to every church that compromises with wrong; traitor to every government that oppresses the people."

— **Wendell Phillips**

The search for the ideal place has been my Holy Grail, but I've never found it. Ideal climates attract too many people and result in big government. Southern California is an excellent example.

Even if you stay in one of the places I mentioned, the heavy hand of government will soon pressure you. Permanent residence means taxes, licenses and the threat of new laws. Your paradise will soon grow sour.

The best solution is to stay mobile and flit from place to place. That way, you can savor many of the freedoms in these unique areas without paying the price that a stationary life exacts.

11

Retirement

"Rest is a good thing, but boredom is its brother."

—Voltaire

"What are you going to do about retirement?," someone asked me when I was leaving my job and starting on the road; "You can't live on Social Security."

Sadly, this is the mindset we live with. Today we are more concerned with working for retirement than working for living. In this quest for security, the government has catered to our fears and given us Social Security, health care, and other benefits for the old, in return for tax money and our freedom. We have sold our birthright for a bowl of porridge when we turn 65.

If you want to know how to prepare for retirement, first ask yourself what retirement is. First, retirement is a sudden cessation of work and a transition to a lifestyle where you do what you want. However, Freedom Road living is all about doing what you want. Consequently, there is no need to "quit work" and start enjoying yourself. You are working and having fun already.

Retirement is also thought of as a time when the money you saved can be spent and enjoyed. But, face it, how often did money make you happy when you were younger? Usually it made you miserable because you didn't have enough. If you're retired and not working, do you think you'll have more money or your desires will have declined? With the Freedom Road life, you learn the folly of counting on money for happiness. It's better to learn it now than when you're old.

Retirement is also the time people plan on traveling and doing what they want. But why should people sacrifice for their whole life just to have a few years of happiness? The best life is one where each day is a joy and we aren't deferring it for some unknown future. With the Freedom Road lifestyle, you're living and enjoying each day. With the skills you learned in this book, you can make your future as pleasant as the present.

The most important skill you must acquire is self confidence. People are afraid of old age because they have little faith in their ability to cope. They assume they will be too sick, too poor, and too senile to survive. As a result, they save money as a futile protection against these possibilities. But they never ask if money helps a senile, sick person. It may bring more attention, but life in a nursing home is still miserable. In fact, if you have money, your relatives or the government are more likely to force you into a nursing home. If you're poor, no one will care to foot the bill for your care.

So try to develop your confidence. The Freedom Road lifestyle gives you many of the skills you can use to live a full life as you grow older. Use them, and your life will be just as fulfilling when you grow old.

Old Age Skills

"It doesn't take a majority to make a rebellion; it takes only a few determined leaders and a sound cause."

— **H.L. Mencken**

Health

Nothing scares people more than the illnesses that come with growing old. With our government-controlled-medical system, health care is too expensive for even the rich. Unfortunately, most retired people want mandated government health care. They never stop to realize that bureaucrats will do to their bodies what they did to the Post Office.

The real solution to improved heath care is to start living a better, healthier life today — while you're young. Fortunately, the Freedom Road lifestyle helps because most inexpensive food is also nutritious. These foods will make you reach your natural weight and feel better.

Another advantage of your new lifestyle is the opportunity to engage in healthy activities. With the free time, you can take up an activity like walking, swimming, or a sport. The additional exercise will keep you fit and help avoid many problems that come with a sedentary life.

The final health tip is to avoid stress. Doctors tell us that stress, often caused by traditional work, acts like a long term poison to our cardiovascular system. If we can avoid the troubles that plague us in the traditional world, our blood pressure will be lower, our heart will work less, and it will give us many more years of good service.

Lower Costs

Old age means a reduced earning level. But, as we have shown, a Freedom Road lifestyle is so inexpensive that the average person can continue to live well on a small or non-existent pension. By learning to keep costs low when we're young, we learn how to be happy on less money and we avoid the shock of reduced income when we become older.

Keep Working

There is a myth that we have to stop working when we're 65. That was started by FDR to drive older Americans out of the work force during the Depression. Of course, his ideas didn't help us recover from the Depression, and they aren't helping the retired today.

If you hate your job, you're probably looking forward to retiring at 65 so you can leave the office. But what are you going to do? Do you realize that the rest of your life is now dependent on the whims of the company pension manager and the politicians in Washington? What may seem like a secure retirement could explode in your face.

If you enjoy your work, there is no reason to quit. If you continue to work, you keep yourself physically and mentally active and you don't become a hostage to the people who control your pension. Of course, you may want to change your workload as you grow older, but that choice is yours, not someone else's.

Continue Learning

Some unfortunate souls think that learning is for the young and someone who isn't working doesn't need to study. That's wrong. I don't know about the rest of you, but I intend to keep learning until the day I die.

One of the sad misconceptions of old age is that senility is inevitable. In fact, studies show that intelligence can increase as you grow older — as long as you continue to exercise your mind. If you continue to learn and challenge your mind, the chances of becoming senile are less.

There are many older Americans who return to college after they retire, but that's an expensive choice. Since the goal at college is to acquire a piece of paper for finding a job, the older American can forget the cost of a formal education. If the knowledge, not the sheepskin, is what you want, there is a cheaper method for learning you can take on the road with you.

Visit one of the used bookstores near a university. There you will find a wide selection of used textbooks on subjects you never imagined. Carefully look over the books and find a couple on subjects you like and can understand. Buy them and take them home to study. Since most professors teach out of the textbook, you can learn just as much as if you attended the classes.

I use this technique when I need to bone up on a subject for a writing assignment. I've found that a couple of days of intense study can equal the learning from a one semester class (in college this is called cramming). Inevitably, my articles are more insightful when I spend a little time studying the subject. Even if I have the opportunity to interview an expert, I can spend the time asking detailed questions instead of simplistic ones.

When you finish studying your book, why not try to write a "term paper" on the subject? You may be able to find a newsletter or local paper that will print it. Even if you just give it to a friend to read and critique, you will have learned something and kept your mind active.

Saving For Retirement

During most of this book, I've talked about limiting your savings, but there are times when you want something set aside. Unfortunately, the government has regulated the investment field in order to find additional tax money, so it's harder than before to save money on the road.

The best savings for the Freedom Road lifestyle is food. If you read the chapter on food, you know that a hundred dollars will buy enough beans and rice to last two people for a year. Therefore, it makes sense to buy enough food to last about a year. That way, should an emergency arise, at least you can eat and use your food budget for other items.

Precious metals offer an excellent long term savings for someone living on the Freedom Road. Although prices have varied considerably over the years, they remain an excellent store of value. In other words, the amount of rice an ounce of gold buys today will be close to the amount of rice it bought a century ago and what it will buy in another 20 years.

Precious metals are mobile and you can travel without remaining in contact with your broker. They also offer the same tax advantages of an IRA: you don't have to pay taxes on any profits until you sell them.

If you do save precious metals, you should keep a variety for different uses. One ounce silver coins can be used for small transactions (many small businesses will accept precious metals instead of money) while different sizes of gold coins will be good for larger transactions.

Gold and silver prices are volatile, so it makes sense to establish a long term savings program instead of making one large purchase. If, as a young person, you save about $50 a month in precious metals, your average price will be low and you will have a nest egg that will cover most needs.

Summary

"Society is a madhouse whose wardens are the officials and the police."

— **August Strindberg**

Retirement shouldn't bother someone living a Freedom Road lifestyle because they're already enjoying themselves. The healthier lifestyle should limit medical problems. Nor is money a problem, because their needs are simpler and they have learned to make money while having fun. I guess you can say Freedom Road is a way to retire when you're in your twenties.

12

Freedom Road As
An Ideal Sabbatical

"Adventure is not outside a man; it is within."

— **David Grayson**

Maybe Freedom Road interests you, but you enjoy your job or you don't know if you want a permanent life on the road. On the other hand, you want a little more adventure in life, you need a break from your job, and you want to travel. Well, why not take a Freedom Road sabbatical?

Taking long vacations is common everywhere but the United States and Japan. College professors take every seventh year off in order to study and take a break from classes. In Europe, month long vacations are normal, especially in August, and longer ones are not uncommon. American workers are expected to refresh themselves with one or two week vacations. As a result, most vacations are hurried affairs and people often return from them in need of a rest. But, what's worse, they haven't had a chance to improve themselves spiritually or mentally. They have merely taken a "junk food" break: bulk, not substance.

If you need a longer vacation to relax and improve yourself, why not use the Freedom Road lifestyle? With careful planning, you can take an unpaid sabbatical and not make a major dent in your savings. You can use the time to travel, relax, maybe even improve yourself with study. Even if you go back to a conventional world, at least Freedom Road provided you with that ideal vacation.

Taking Time Off

A long vacation is great, but how do you convince your boss to let you take the time off? It's easier than you think, especially if you take a sabbatical without pay (remember, the Freedom Road lifestyle is inexpensive enough to allow you to live without a salary). Here are a few hints for taking a sabbatical.

Quit

The most popular time to take a long vacation is between jobs. Many new employers will let you report late, so you can take a few months to travel and relax. In fact, if the two jobs are in different cities, you can pack your goods in the RV (if you don't have many belongings) and take them along with you. That way, any reimbursement for the move will also help defray the cost of your vacation. If you have too many goods, have a moving company transfer them to storage in the new city and just travel with the necessities. Most companies will reimburse you for moving your dependents and vehicles, so you should have some compensation for your trip. The RV can even act as a residence while you are "house shopping" in the new city (you may even decide to live in it permanently).

Work Slowdown

Every business has a slow period and most employers hate firing anyone during these times. If you approach your boss and offer to take an unpaid vacation, he or she may thank you. This method will also protect you from any layoffs during your vacation because terminating you would save little money for management. In fact, in a numbers game where management is trying to fire the fewest people while saving the most money, you may be one of the only remaining workers.

Taking a sabbatical during a work slowdown allows you to retain certain benefits (like insurance), and a generous employer may even give you a small payment to help defray costs.

Time Off Without Pay

Most large companies have a policy of time off without pay. This is often used by pregnant women, students, and people with serious illnesses. However, if your job can be covered, most employers will let you take the time off for other reasons. One of the advantages is that you keep your benefits and often the time still counts toward seniority and retirement.

If your employer says you're too important and he won't give you the time off, consider quitting. If you're that valuable, another company will probably be willing to hire you for more money. Then you can take a sabbatical between jobs.

Professional Improvement

Knowledge is growing so fast that many professionals are failing to keep up with the changes. Although most companies don't give paid time off for professional enrichment, they will often grant time off without pay for something professionally oriented. If your sabbatical is couched in a professional way (time to write a paper or book, study somewhere, or see something), your employer will probably grant your wish. One of the advantages of a professional improvement sabbatical is that you may become more valuable for your employer and your pay may increase when you return.

Work on the Road

Most employers hate to admit this, but with the computer and phone lines, people can work anywhere they want including an RV. If you're too important to stop working, you want to keep receiving paychecks, and your work can be done on the road, why not try this approach? If your employer is open-minded or you can push him into a corner, he may agree. If your work requires some travel inside the US, he may even like the idea of a part-time worker visiting customers around the country.

Planning A Sabbatical

Since you will probably forego a regular paycheck, you should carefully plan your sabbatical. As a rule, the planning period should be just as long as your vacation.

If you intend to stay away for one year, therefore, you should start planning about one year ahead. That will give you time to arrange your finances, settle your job situation, and start practicing your new lifestyle. With proper planning, your vacation will be enjoyable and your finances will be better when you return.

Eliminate Debt

A successful sabbatical has the same requirement as a successful Freedom Road life; you must eliminate debt. If you're planning your trip a year ahead, you should be able to rid yourself of most debt or at least make early payments so you won't have installment payments due when you're on the road.

One of the benefits of a Freedom Road lifestyle is the clean slate when you return. If you combine that with the cheaper living habits you acquire on the road, you should be able to save money when you return to work.

Save Money

You need money for an RV and living expenses. As I said earlier, there isn't an easy way, so you just have to use payroll deductions and self discipline. If you don't have the discipline, try to find a way to make money on the road. One suggestion is selling at flea markets. The skills are easily acquired, it only requires a few days a week and you have unlimited travel possibilities.

Learn the Inexpensive Lifestyle

The sooner you start living inexpensively, the sooner you can save money and eliminate debt. With any type of luck, you can lose some weight and get in better shape before you go.

Eliminate Housing Costs

Have you been thinking about changing houses or moving from your apartment? Why not tie that into your sabbatical? Not only do you eliminate your mortgage or rent, you also cut your water, phone, heating, gas, electricity, property tax, cable, garbage, and maintenance costs. Probably more than half your monthly expenses would disappear if you moved out of your housing and put your belongings in storage. Remember, you're living in an RV and there isn't any reason to keep that house anyway.

Buying an RV

Buying an RV for a sabbatical is different from buying one to live in permanently. Since you will use it for a short period, you may want to consider the resale value more. Depending on the condition of the vehicle, the time of the year, and the care you take of it, you could break even or even make money when the time comes to sell it.

Since you will only be living in it for a short period of time, you can save money by buying a smaller RV than necessary for a permanent Freedom Road lifestyle. For instance, sabbaticals of 3 to 6 months could use a truck camper or a van conversion while something bigger would be necessary for longer vacations. One advantage of the smaller RV is that you can travel more places than people with larger vehicles.

Summary

"A little rebellion now and then... is a medicine necessary for the sound health of government."

— **Thomas Jefferson**

Freedom Road offers an unprecedented opportunity to take that once-in-a-lifetime sabbatical. Many people have taken time from work and spent little money in the process. The result is a wonderful experience and usually an improved attitude toward work. Everyone needs a break, and if you're lucky, you'll never return.

13

Freedom From Illness

"He who has health, has hope; and he who has hope has everything."

— **Arabian Proverb**

The body is a Ferrari and modern life is like the Los Angeles freeway at rush hour. Small, healthy habits, like eating oat bran once a week, will do little more for your total health than balancing tires regularly will help the Ferrari on the freeway.

The body, like the Ferrari, was made to run. It's uncomfortable idling at a desk, consuming the wrong fuel, or not running all-out. But, modern life is a package of everything that leads us to an early grave. We eat too much of the wrong foods, we don't have the time to exercise, we live in polluted big cities, and we try to cope with stress. No wonder our bodies are in lousy shape.

Unfortunately, civilization doesn't have an effective answer to these problems. Fads like jogging come and go because we don't have the time to do what we want, much less sweat. We only eat healthy food as long as it tastes good and it's the "in thing" to eat. And, we live in a world where stress denotes success.

By breaking away from the world, however, you can eliminate many of the problems that lead to illness in our society and live a better, healthier life on the road. For instance, stress is usually caused by job pressures or money concerns. In the Freedom Road lifestyle, your needs are simple and the stress from a job is non-existent.

Another advantage of this lifestyle is the opportunity to leave the pollution of the cities and live in a cleaner environment. According to an EPA study, over half of US citizens live in cities with too much smog and one third live in areas with dangerously high carbon monoxide. While most people can't do anything about it because they're tied to their job or house, the person who lives in an RV can pick up and move to a healthier place. For instance, we used to stay in Las Vegas, but the brown haze that obscured the mountains always disturbed me. Now I'm staying where the air is so clean I can see small buildings on a mountain thirty miles away. As a result, my wife, who suffers from asthma, is taking less medication and feeling better.

A freer lifestyle also gives you the time to take better care of yourself. How many times did you want to join a health spa or exercise but you didn't have the time? On

Freedom Road, I can exercise when I want. In fact, when I have writer's block, I often exercise just to get back into the mood for writing.

Finally, as we mentioned earlier, a simpler life means eating cheaper, better food that allows you to lose weight. Since some doctors say each extra pound of weight subtracts one month from your life, Freedom Road can make life not only healthier, but longer. When we consider the money people spend to extend their lives a few months, we realize the Freedom Road lifestyle makes us richer than we can imagine.

Finding Doctors

You're in a new city and sick. You look in the Yellow Pages and call some doctors, but they usually can't see you for a few days. What are you going to do? If you need medical attention and it isn't an emergency room case, ask the doctor's receptionist if you can come and wait for an open spot. Since many doctors give themselves a little slack in their schedule, by waiting in the office, you have a good chance to see the doctor for a few minutes between patients or when there's a cancellation.

Here are some other suggestions for finding doctors in a new city:

Referral Service

Many large cities operate a doctor referral service. Usually it's paid for by a hospital or a doctors' group and tries to match needs with available doctors. The referral service is free and you can even use them for specialists. If you need the phone number, check the phone book or call a nearby hospital.

Hotel or RV Park Doctor

Hotels and places that have tourists often have a local doctor who will handle patients. However, the treatment by a resort physician may not reflect your needs. For instance, he may try to control your symptoms during your stay and assume you'll go home to your regular doctor. The treatment may only be temporary and not solve the problem.

Referral from Another Doctor

If you have a regular doctor in one place, ask him to recommend a doctor where you are going. He may have a school buddy in the area or know of a qualified specialist. Generally the doctor will give you a good recommendation, and the previous relationship will help if you need to have your medical records forwarded.

Cheap Medicine In Mexico

When my wife was visiting a doctor in Arizona, he recommended a pharmacy in Mexico fill the prescription. Not only was the medicine better than that in the US, it was considerably cheaper.

Doctors and lawyers haven't had the opportunity to ruin the medical system of Mexico, so any time you're near the border, you might want to park in the US and cross the border to stock up the medicine chest. This is an excellent suggestion for anyone taking a regular medicine and is legal as long as you are buying the medicine for your own use. Here are some advantages.

Prices

Usually, everything is cheaper in Mexico, but the difference between Mexican and American drugs is astounding. The lower cost of overhead and the difference in liability law makes medicine affordable for the average person. If you have a long term illness that requires regular dosages of medicine, a trip south of the border will be well worth it.

Less Need for Prescriptions

In the US, you visit a doctor who writes a prescription. You take it to a drug store where the pharmacist (who is little more than a repackager) fills the order. Even if you know what's wrong, you must see and pay the doctor before you can expect any relief. That not only makes health care more expensive, but it doesn't help on Sunday night when you have a bad cough.

The Mexican Pharmacist is a professional who has a greater part in the health care of Mexicans than the US druggist. Unless you're really in poor health, you ask the pharmacist what he recommends for certain problems. He will then sell the product to you without the necessity of a prescription.

As a result of this enlightened system, you can buy ethical drugs over the counter in Mexico that you wouldn't be able to acquire in the US except with an expensive doctor appointment. Both you and your wallet are better off.

New Medicine

The FDA is more concerned with maintaining its control over the pharmaceutical industry and creating paperwork than with healing people. As a result, many worthwhile medications are unknown in the US. A quick trip to a

Mexican drug store will offer many drugs that are common throughout the world, but the US government wants to prevent you from taking.

Alternative Treatments

Doctors are a traditional lot and most think of healing in terms of surgery or drugs. Like past medical giants, such as Pasteur, some doctors are challenging conventional wisdom and treating patients without cutting or chemicals. Since the US medical establishment is powerful, many of these practices aren't allowed in the US but are available in Mexico.

If you're tired of traditional medicine and don't think it's helping you, try a clinic south of the border. Of course, the freedom to try alternatives also includes the responsibility to make the right choice. Be sure you pick carefully.

Free Medicine

The drug industry in the United States is a multi-billion dollar business that's just as competitive as fast food. However, instead of advertising on TV, most drug companies use representatives who visit doctors to push the latest discoveries.

To develop a long term source of revenue, these representatives try to push medicine that must be taken regularly for long periods (heart medication is a good example). They leave samples of these medications for the doctor to give to patients when they prescribe it. Some physicians forget about the samples and inevitably throw them away.

Next time you visit your doctor, ask him for any free samples of medication you're taking. Usually they're glad to oblige and if you're the only one who asked or the representative just visited, you may leave the office with weeks of free medicine worth more than you spent on the visit. If you know the nurse, you can find out when the drug representative visits and time your appointment. Who knows, maybe they'll let you just drop by without an appointment?

Veterinary Medicines

Medical care consists of two factors: knowledge and supplies. If you have the knowledge to handle small emergencies, you can acquire the supplies at the local animal supply store.

Veterinary medical supplies are readily available at many stores, especially in small towns and in the country. Although they're cheaper, these medicines come from the same lots given to humans and have the same purity (the difference in price reflects the added cost of liability laws and bureaucratic regulation). With the exception of a few medicines like pain killers, you can walk in and purchase them over the counter without any paperwork.

If you want to treat yourself, it's important to know what you're doing. There are a couple of books in *Appendix II* that will help in diagnosing and treating people.

Summary

"*An oppressed people are authorized whenever they can to rise and break their fetters.*"

— **Henry Clay**

The greatest gift we've received from the Freedom Road lifestyle is health. We feel better with the simple foods we eat and the life we lead has made us healthier. Our fitness has also helped us break another bond with government. We no longer depend on the government granted doctors' monopoly, nor are we willing to turn over our health to the government in return for lower medical costs. Our bodies, as well as our minds, are our own.

14

Going Down The Road

"As long as the world shall last there will be wrongs, and if no man objected and no man rebelled, those wrongs would last forever."

— **Clarence Darrow**

We are at the end of the book, but not at the end of Freedom Road. Centuries ago, our forefathers left a comfortable life to seek the freedom of the wilderness. In the future, people will leave earth and space colonies to seek the freedom of the next unexplored star or the depths of space, because the search for freedom from society and government will be a never ending one until human beings realize that controlling the actions of another is wrong.

These new members of Freedom Road will have different technologies and different worries, but they will not be that different from us. They will have chosen that path because they realize true freedom comes from knowing how to survive without relying on government.

Like us, they will know freedom comes from invulnerability to threats; a government that can't find them in the cold, limitless recesses of space can't threaten them. And in that unpopulated space they will realize money is just a tool for happiness, not a goal.

But, most important, they will realize true freedom comes not from the size of the universe or the size of the fuel tank, but is found in the limitless spaces of the mind.

Appendix I

Recipes For Cheap,

Healthy Living

Even if you never go out on Freedom Road, these recipes will save hundreds of dollars and improve your health. Many are from pioneer days, when money was dear and people had the time to prepare good food. I hope you enjoy them as much as I have.

BEANS AND RICE CASSEROLE

This is a great meal for dollar a day living and a good place to put any leftovers. Beans and rice also provide a balanced protein diet.

1 onion
1 clove garlic
1 cup pinto beans (cooked)
1 cup rice
¼ cup grated cheese (cheddar, longhorn, or swiss)

Add onions, rice, beans, 2½ cups of water, and garlic to a casserole dish and cook until the rice is done. Add the cheese, stir and cook for another 5 minutes. Serves three.

BURRITO

This is one of my favorites and another good way to live on a dollar a day.

2 cups pinto beans
1 tablespoon chili powder
¼ teaspoon crushed red pepper
2 medium yellow onions
2 cloves garlic
Grated cheese
Flour tortillas
¼ pound bacon ends
¼ cup corn meal

Soak the beans overnight in water, chili powder, pepper, and the garlic. The next day, add water until the beans are covered, cover the pan and cook slowly for two hours. The beans will be cooked when they are soft. Add the corn meal and cook for another half hour.

Dice and cook ¼ pound of bacon. When it's cooked, add two onions and continue heating until the onions are sauteed. Mash the beans and add to the bacon and onions. When mixed, remove from the heat.

To serve, spoon some beans into a tortilla, add some grated cheese, and fold. You can also add salsa, guacamole, or lettuce. Serves four.

CHOP SUEY

This is another good recipe for keeping food costs below $1 a day. Thanks to Bill Kaysing and his book *The Senior Citizens' Survival Manual* for this recipe.

4 cups of sprouted Mung beans
2 onions
1 stalk of celery
2 cloves garlic
Mushrooms
Left over beef, chicken or pork

Cook meat (if any) in a frying pan. Then add chopped onions, minced garlic, and chopped celery and cook until tender. Add bean sprouts and mushrooms (if desired) and cook until done.

Serve with soy sauce.

COLCANNON

This is an Irish dish that kept many of their poor alive.

6 medium potatoes, peeled
    (Chop up the peels and leave in the dish)
1 onion
1½ cups carrots or other root vegetable
½ cup milk
2 tablespoons butter or margarine

Boil potatoes until tender, drain, and mash. Boil the onion and vegetables until tender. Add milk and butter to the mashed potatoes and season to taste, then beat them until fluffy. Add the vegetables and onion and serve.

COTTAGE CHEESE

If you're staying in the country near a source of inexpensive whole milk, you can make your own cottage cheese with little effort.

1 quart whole milk
2 tablespoons lemon juice

Heat the milk to scalding, but do not boil. Set the milk aside and add the lemon juice. Separate the solids from the whey by pouring the mixture through a strainer lined with cheese cloth. Let it drain for a couple hours and store in a refrigerator. Save the whey and use it with powdered milk to add more body.

You can make a nice herb cheese to spread on bread or crackers by adding herbs like garlic, green onions, etc. to the curds.

FRIED BREAD

This is a quick way to make bread with only a frying pan. It was a staple of the Navajo.

2 cups flour
2 teaspoons baking powder
½ teaspoon salt
½ cup powdered milk

Mix flour, baking powder, salt, and powdered milk. Add a little warm water to make dough. Knead it until the dough is soft but not sticky. Let stand for two hours while covered with a cloth. Shape into 2 inch balls and then flatten them into a circle about 8 inches in diameter. Fry in a large pan with a half inch of shortening or oil. The oil is hot enough when a piece of dough turns brown. Fry the bread until brown and flip over.

HEALTHY GRAVY

If you like gravy, but want to avoid the calories or cholesterol, here's a substitute for you.

½ cup pinto beans
2 beef bullion cubes

Dissolve the bullion in 1 cup water and soak the beans in it overnight. Add water and cook the beans until done. Draw off the water and use it as gravy. If you want more thickness, add flour or mash up some beans. Season with garlic or salt and pepper as desired.

HARDTACK

This recipe was given to me by a gold prospector. Not only is the bread cheap, it's filling and lasts for days. This was often the only bread many pioneers ate in the wilderness.

2 cups whole wheat flour
2 tablespoons oil

Add enough water to the flour to make a dough. Add oil to a frying pan and heat. Shape the dough into disks 3 inches in diameter and about ½ inch thick. Place the dough into the pan and cook until the outside is a golden brown.

Although the uses for hardtack are limitless, one of the best ways to eat it is hot with a piece of cheese on top. You can make corn dodgers (remember John Wayne in *True Grit*) by using corn meal instead of whole wheat.

MUSH

This is cheap and sticks to your ribs. It's only limited by your imagination.

2 cups corn meal
1 teaspoon salt
4 cups water

Slowly add the corn meal to the boiling salted water while stirring. Let it cook for a few minutes without letting the mixture burn. You can serve it by adding milk and sugar or you can let it sit overnight in a greased loaf pan and you can cut, slice, and fry it. When fried, serve with butter and syrup.

If you add ½ a pound of sausage and 1 onion, let it sit overnight in a greased loaf pan, you have scrapple.

MEXICAN CASSEROLE

Another dollar a day meal.

3 cups cooked pinto beans
2 tomatoes
½ green pepper
1 clove garlic
1 onion
1 teaspoon chili powder
4 strips of bacon

Mince the vegetables and garlic and combine all the ingredients except the bacon in a casserole dish. Place the bacon on the top. Bake at 350° for an hour.

OATMEAL CROQUETTES
This really sticks to your ribs.
1 cup rolled oats
¾ cup hot milk
1 egg
1 onion
½ cup oil
Soak the oats in milk for an hour to soften them. Add the egg, chopped onion, and any salt and pepper you want. Heat the oil in a pan and drop spoonfuls of the mixture in the pan. Brown both sides and serve.

ONION SALAD
If you want a salad to add zest to your meal, but you don't have greens you can try this.
2 onions
vinegar
sugar
salt
pepper
Finely mince the onions and add the rest of the ingredients to taste. Let sit overnight.

PINTO BEAN FUDGE
The pioneers used pinto beans for everything. Here's proof.
2/3 cup canned milk
1 2/3 cups sugar
1½ cups diced marshmallows
½ cup chopped nuts
½ cup cooked pinto beans
1½ cups chocolate chips
1 teaspoon vanilla

Combine sugar and milk in a pan and boil for five minutes while stirring constantly. Add the other ingredients and stir until the marshmallows dissolve. Pour in a buttered pan and let cool before cutting into squares.

PINTO BEAN LOAF
This is like meat loaf, but you use beans instead of hamburger.

4 cups of cooked pinto beans
** (soak overnight and cook two hours)**
2 green peppers
1 small onion
1 cup bread crumbs
2 eggs (beaten)
Milk

Mash the beans and finely mince the green peppers and onions before mixing them together. Add bread crumbs, eggs, and season with salt and pepper. Add just enough milk to hold the mixture together. Place in a loaf pan and bake about 50 minutes in a moderate oven. Serve with hot tomato sauce and grated cheese.

PINTO BEAN SOUP
This is a great soup for leftovers.

3 cups of uncooked pinto beans
1 onion
2 stalks celery
3 tomatoes
Meat scraps (preferably ham)
1 clove garlic

Cook beans, minced garlic, and meat scraps together in water until the beans are soft. Dice the vegetables and add. Season to taste. Add other vegetables if you want.

POTATO SOUP

This is a hearty meal on a cold afternoon and fits the dollar a day limit. You can also add other leftovers to this.

4 potatoes
4 slices of bacon and grease
1 onion
1 cup powdered milk
1 tablespoon butter or margarine
 season to taste

Chop the potatoes and boil until soft. Fry bacon and saute onions in grease. Mash half of the potatoes and then add all the ingredients to a quart of water and stir. Cook until ready.

RICE CASSEROLE

Another dollar a day meal. It's filling and I can't see how you could gain weight on it.

1 cup brown rice
2½ cups water
2 cubes of bullion
1 onion
½ green pepper
Any other meat or vegetable leftovers

Dissolve bullion in water and add rice, chopped peppers, onions, and other ingredients. Bake or microwave until the rice is done. Serve with soy sauce. This is also good with a ½ cup of sprouted mung beans.

SPROUTING SEEDS

Learn this and you can have fresh salads and greens all the time for next to nothing.

Seeds (alfalfa, wheat, mung beans, etc.)
Jar with top (punch holes in the top)

Wash seeds and let them soak overnight. Next morning, drain them and rinse them thoroughly. Then put them in a dark, warm place. Continue this routine twice a day until they are ready.

SPROUT SALAD

I was staying in a plywood shack in the arctic tundra when I had an urge for a salad. The nearest head of lettuce was 75 miles away, so I made this up.

4 cups various sprouts
   (alfalfa, mung beans, etc.)
¼ cup oil
½ cup vinegar
1 clove minced garlic
Bacon bits
Grated or diced cheese

Mix sprouts, bacon, garlic, and cheese together. Just before serving, add the oil and vinegar together and pour over the sprouts. Add any other raw vegetables like carrots or onions if you have them.

WESTERN BAKED BEANS

Why use this as a side dish when it makes a great main course?

2 cups pinto beans
1 clove garlic
2 small onions
½ cup brown sugar or molasses
1 teaspoon chili powder
1 finely chopped tomato
4 slices of bacon or ham

Soak the beans overnight. Add the garlic and simmer for an hour. Remove the water and set aside. Add the whole onions to the beans, sprinkle with the sugar and chili, add the tomato, add 1 cup of the water you cooked the beans in, and put the bacon on top. Bake in the oven for 5 hours at 300 degrees.

WHEAT CASSEROLE

Wheat is a cheap grain and can be used as a rice substitute.

1 cup wheat, soaked overnight
3 tomatoes
1 onion
½ cup grated cheese
2 cloves garlic
salt and oregano

Cook the wheat with the chopped tomatoes until the wheat is tender. Mince the garlic, chop the onion and add to the casserole along with the salt and oregano. Cook until the onions are tender. Add the cheese on top and bake in the oven until the cheese is bubbling. Serve with soy sauce.

One key to eating inexpensively is to develop your own recipes. These are just a few ideas for meals that still cost less than a dollar a day. As you spend more time cooking and learn which ingredients work for you, you can start developing your own favorites.

Appendix II

More Information

There's more to living a free lifestyle, living without a regular job, hints for inexpensive living, and RV life than I could ever cover in one book. The following books are excellent additions to your library if you're seriously seeking the Freedom Road lifestyle.

Ecotopian Encyclopedia For The 80s, Ernest Callenbach, And/Or Press, Berkeley, CA.

This is a wonderful reference to alternative lifestyles that shows you how to live better for less. It was written in 1981, so some material is dated, but it has many timeless suggestions on inexpensive living and survival in an era where inflation is rampant and the ecology is threatened.

Home Is Where You Park It, Kay Peterson, RoVing Press, Estes Park, CO.

This is a good, practical book written by present day nomads. It gives you solid advice on selecting an RV, moving into it, and living in it.

How To Live In The New America, William Kaysing, Prentice-Hall, Englewood Cliffs, NJ.

Bill Kaysing started living a freer life when everyone else was trying to buy a Cadillac with fins. This book tells you how to leave the suburbs and cities and move to the country. He tells you how to find inexpensive land, make solid homes for about $100, and where to find healthy food.

How To Make Cash Money Selling At Swap Meets, Flea Markets, Etc., Jordan Cooper, Loompanics Unlimited, Port Townsend, WA.

If you want to travel and make money at swap meets, this book will get you started. It covers everything from buying merchandise to finding the best spots at the shows.

How To Survive Without A Salary, Charles Long, Summerhill Press Ltd., Toronto.

This book describes all the facets of living a good life even though you don't have a regular job or salary.

The Best Book Catalog In The World, Loompanics Unlimited, Port Townsend, WA.

This is the ultimate reference for the freedom seeker, with books on all aspects of achieving more freedom. Many of the books recommended in this Appendix are available through Loompanics Unlimited.

Merck Manual, Merck Sharp & Dohme Research Laboratories, Rahway. NJ.

It was first published in 1899 and is now in its fourteenth edition. It's the most widely used medical text and is the standard text for all medical professionals. It covers all medical disorders from abdominojugular reflux to zoophilia, their symptoms and recommended treatments. Although written for the medical professional, the educated amateur can understand it. This is a must for anyone who wants to rely on themselves for medical care.

Paradise Found, R. Emil Neuman, United Research Publishers, Leucadia, CA.

This book tells how to live in North America for under $300 a month.

Recreational Vehicles, Bill Alderman, Bonus Books, Chicago, IL.

This book tells you how to find the best buys in RVs. It lists popular options, tells about choices, and even describes how appliances work. We owe our nice RV to the information in this book.

Simple Living Investments, Michael Phillips and Catherine Campbell, Clear Glass Publishing, San Francisco, CA.

This is a simple book that looks at what's really important in life and how to translate it into an inexpensive lifestyle.

Senior Citizens' Survival Manual, Bill Kaysing, Bellwether Press, Venice, CA.

This book is too good to be just for senior citizens. In fact, of all the books listed in this Appendix, this one should be the first you buy. He has practical advice on better living that's good even if you don't go on the Freedom Road.

Survivalist's Medicine Chest, Ragnar Benson, Paladin Press, Boulder, CO.

If you want to keep your medical costs down and treat yourself, this is an excellent book. The author learned how to use veterinary medicines to treat people while in Africa.

The Kingdom In The Country, James Conway, Houghton Mifflin, Boston, MA.

An entertaining book about government land in the West and the people who live on it. The author is a statist, so the book advocates more government control, but it provides the freedom seeker with some good ideas for places to live.

Vonu, Edited by Jon Fisher, Loompanics Unlimited, Port Townsend, WA.

A compilation of letters from Rayo, a pioneer in personal freedom. In it, he talks about the theory of freedom and practical tips for becoming invisible to government.

How To Buy Land Cheap, 4th Edition, by Edward Preston, Loompanics Unlimited, Port Townsend, WA.

Revised and updated, this book is considered the Bible of bargain-basement land buying. It contains information to help you step-by-step in finding property, bidding on it, and closing the deal.

Great Hideouts Of The West, by Bill Kaysing, Loompanics Unlimited, Port Townsend, WA.

You never know when you might need a good hideout. Things can change in a hurry — industrial or natural catastrophes, war, collapse of social structures, or just to plain get away. This book presents ideas about the hideout concept so that you can use your own creative imagination to develop the hideout that will be all that you desire.

YOU WILL ALSO WANT TO READ:

☐ **17054 HOW TO BUY LAND CHEAP, 4th Edition,** *by Edward Preston.* Revised and updated, this book is considered the bible of bargain-basement land buying. Contains information to help you step-by-step in finding property, bidding on it, and closing the deal. *1991, 5½ x 8½, 146 pp, illustrated, glossary, soft cover. $14.95.*

☐ **17037 GREAT HIDEOUTS OF THE WEST,** *by Bill Kaysing.* You never know when you might need a good hideout. Things can change in a hurry — industrial or natural catastrophes, war, collapse of social structures, or just to plain get away. This book presents ideas about the hideout concept so that you can use your own creative imagination to develop the hideout that will be all that you desire. *1987, 5½ x 8½, 170 pp, profusely illustrated, soft cover. $9.95.*

☐ **17049 EDEN SEEKERS GUIDE,** *Edited by William Seavey.* This book is a compilation of some of the leading edge thought on place choices to help you find your own personal Eden. It advises where to look, what to look for, and other possible considerations, including important data on each location listed. *1989, 5½ x 8½, 169 pp, soft cover. $12.95.*

☐ **10053 DIRECTORY OF US MAIL DROPS, With An Appendix for Foreign Countries,** *compiled by Michael Hoy.* This comprehensive directory lists over 800 companies all over the world who will rent you an unlisted address for receiving mail, and will forward mail for you. Widely recognized as the best book of its kind — a must for privacy seekers! *1991, 8½ x 11, more than 800 listings, soft cover. $14.95.*

And much more! We offer the very finest in controversial and unusual books — please turn to our catalog announcement on the next page.

_____FR